Easy
Low Carb Living

Simple & Practical
Low Carb Lifestyle Advice

Patricia Haakonson, B.Sc.
Harv Haakonson, M.D.

Book design, typesetting:
Vivencia Resources Group
www.members.shaw.ca/vrg
Cover design: Roy Diment, VRG
Cover photo: Destrube Photography

National Library of Canada Cataloguing in Publication

Haakonson, Patricia, 1950-
        Easy low carb living / Patricia Haakonson and Harv
Haakonson.

Includes index.
ISBN 1-55369-376-0

        1. Low-carbohydrate diet. I. Haakonson, Harv, 1940- II. Title.

RM237.73.H318 2002   613.2'5   C2002-901557-X

TRAFFORD   *PRINTED IN CANADA*

This book was published *on-demand* in cooperation with Trafford Publishing.
On-demand publishing is a unique process and service of making a book available for retail sale to the public taking advantage of on-demand manufacturing and Internet marketing.
On-demand publishing includes promotions, retail sales, manufacturing, order fulfilment, accounting and collecting royalties on behalf of the author.

Suite 6E, 2333 Government St., Victoria, B.C. V8T 4P4, CANADA
Phone   250-383-6864   Toll-free   1-888-232-4444 (Canada & US)
Fax   250-383-6804   E-mail   sales@trafford.com
Web site   www.trafford.com   TRAFFORD PUBLISHING IS A DIVISION OF TRAFFORD HOLDINGS LTD.
Trafford Catalogue #02-0189   www.trafford.com/robots/02-0189.html

10   9   8   7   6   5   4   3

CONTENTS

FOREWORD

A Life Changing Experience

S hortly before my 50th Birthday, I resolved to lose the extra 25 pounds that I had managed to accumulate over the previous 15 years. Not an earth shattering decision, but one that would change my life forever!

I was semi-retired at age 49, and enjoying some long awaited travel and work on my golf game. I was vacationing in California when I made this momentous decision, thus it was that I saw an ad in the local newspaper for a Doctor Platt. This ad promised to teach me to 'turn on' my metabolism to lose weight. This thought appealed to me (as it was designed to) for I had tried all the other 'diet fixes' to no avail. None of my previous attempts had worked for any extended period of time. I could lose weight (or some of it) by scrimping on meals for a short period, but it always came back. I am not someone who overindulges at meals. I had tried for many years to follow the generally accepted low fat approach to diet. All this accomplished was to add extra pounds.

I consulted Dr. Platt, and to my absolute horror, he suggested that I take a "low carbohydrate" approach to eating. "Is this anything like that Dr. Atkins Diet?" I asked. He assured me it was not. He advised me that it was a similar, but modified approach to low carbohydrate eating. He suggested that I might even realize some positive side effects if I cut down on the amount of carbohydrates I ate.

Like so many other people, I HATE to diet! I love food! I love to bake and cook! Previous attempts had demonstrated that being on a diet makes me feel deprived. This feeling inevitably results in my becoming grumpy, miserable and generally out of sorts. Not a happy prospect for me, or my husband.

I was determined to lose the weight this time. I decided on a two week trial period to test this theory of weight loss. I followed the doctor's recommendations and gave up my beloved breads, bagels, potatoes, and pasta. Within one week I experienced such dramatic changes in my health, that I determined I would never go back to eating the way I used to. It's hard to imagine that at 50 years of age a simple change in diet can have such a far reaching and elemental effect on one's life.

Two significant changes in my health became apparent. I suddenly had more energy than I had when I was a young woman in my 20's. I could be active all day long at any activity and not get tired. "Is this how the rest of the world feels?" I wondered. I no longer felt groggy, tired or sleepy in the middle of the day. Before changing my diet, I had always had difficulty with low energy levels. My husband and I often joked about the bad genes in my family that led me to be a person who had little or no energy after dinner, or sometimes needed a nap in the middle of the afternoon.

The second dramatic change was nothing short of miraculous. The symptoms of a bowel disease, called colitis, that I have suffered from since I was 18 years old, completely disappeared. The symptoms have not returned in more than 2 years. After just one week on the low carb diet, I adopted a low carb approach to eating as a lifestyle choice.

Did I lose the weight? Absolutely! Have I kept it off in the intervening years? You betcha! This fact takes a back seat to the important lessons learned about how we metabolize foods and how they impact every aspect of our lives and our health. We have all heard the old adage "You are what you eat", but I have experienced first hand the absolute truth of this fact.

Deciding to continue eating low carb foods as a lifestyle, (not to lose any more weight but to remain healthy and energetic) demanded that I find a way to make my meals more appealing and flavorful. After doing some research I determined that I had only myself to rely on. With this idea in mind, I set about to write a cookbook. I enjoyed 18 months of creativity while developing and testing recipes for my cookbook. I continued to feel more healthy and energetic than I had for years. I decided to share my discoveries with friends and family.

What started out as a personal project to provide more variety in my diet, turned into an amazing journey into the world of publishing, book selling and media relations. I can no longer call myself retired. I am now a published author! The work required to maintain the momentum created since publishing *Everyday Low Carb Cooking*, (now available in a slightly revised second edition and titled *Easy Low Carb Cooking*) is almost constant. And here I am writing a second, companion book about low carb lifestyles!

I am having the time of my life! I am sharing important information with a wide audience whom I would never have encountered, were it not for that simple decision to lose some weight. I am healthier than I was 30 years ago. I am daring to try things that I might have thought impossible a short while ago – like writing a second book! I am contemplating a full year of travel to promote my books. Retirement is a thing of the past and perhaps the future. My present is full of robust health and crazy, fun ideas.

Welcome to my world!

Patricia Haakonson

CHAPTER 1

Introduction

"Be careful about reading health books.
You may die of a misprint."
Mark Twain

We decided to write this book for a number of reasons, but perhaps the most compelling was the opportunity to share our accumulated knowledge and experience with others who may be interested in low carbohydrate lifestyles. When Patricia first embarked on her modified low carb diet to lose weight, we knew almost nothing about this approach to foods and meal planning. We certainly didn't know about the health implications of eating a high carbohydrate diet. We didn't know where to go for information or for help. We struggled to adapt and adjust our eating habits and to search out low carb products and resources.

We learned through extensive research, reading and trial and error. We made lots of mistakes – some funny, some costly – but learn we did! Harv immersed himself in the medical research to re-educate himself about metabolism, the insulin mechanism and emerging nutrition information. Patricia proceeded to search for low carb ingredients, new low carb products and continue the development of low carb recipes. We both read many of the popular low carb diet books. Some of the diets are consistent with our approach to weight loss, others are not. It was a journey of discovery and intrigue. It was time consuming, often frustrating, and always interesting.

In our reading and research we discovered many of the popular diet books were written in complex scientific terms. Some of the explanations were complicated and difficult to understand. We have made every effort to keep our language simple, and our explanations direct and uncomplicated. You will be the judge of whether we have been successful.

We share with you all we have learned during this period. We also share the strategies we developed that have worked best for us. These strategies have facilitated our dedication to a low carb lifestyle. It has made low carb living *easy* for us. We have included a carbohydrate counter and a food diary so you have all the tools you need to start a low carb lifestyle.

You might ask why we would write another low carb diet book. There are already so many available. Our perspective is that this is not just another diet book. We have not developed an actual 'diet' plan. What we attempt to do is provide a method of weight loss or weight maintenance, using a low carbohydrate approach. We outline other potential health benefits and incorporate the recent radically different recommendations concerning nutrition from Harvard University. We also review some of the popular low carb diet books that are available in bookstores today. We provide the basic tools you need to make things easy for you, should you decide to follow a low carbohydrate lifestyle. We explain how to use these tools in a manner that best suits your needs. We hope we have achieved this using simple language and easy to understand explanations.

North Americans have concentrated on lower fat intake in our diets over the past few decades as the main method of weight control. We now know that this approach has failed miserably. The incidence of adult obesity has reached almost epidemic proportions. Adult onset diabetes, known as Type II diabetes, has dramatically increased over the past ten years. Adolescent obesity is also on the rise with the attendant negative health implications for our young adults. We believe strongly that lowering our carbohydrate consumption is an effective, safe and healthy approach to weight loss and weight maintenance for people of all ages.

We wrote this book partially in response to the many readers of Patricia's cookbook, *Everyday Low Carb Cooking* (now published under the title *Easy Low Carb Cooking*). We have received many e-mail messages with requests for menu planning ideas and questions about 'how to'. We have answered all of these individual requests, and have attempted to represent the overall scope and areas of interest in the chapters of this book. We have received stories from readers about the success of their low carb plans and their delight with the cookbook. Some of these stories are interspersed in the body of this book.

We wanted to round out the information contained in the cookbook with additional new low carb recipes and ideas to make low carb meal preparation easier and quicker. Patricia has developed some amazing new recipes. Some are simple and familiar (Cabbage Rolls) and some are for rare indulgences (Chocolate Mint Cake). All of these new recipes and other ideas are included.

Finally, we were interested in collaborating on a joint project like a book, to which we could contribute equally. Harv brings the credibility of his medical degree and years of practice, as well as his personal experience with low carb lifestyles. Patricia brings her experience in learning to deal with a low carb lifestyle, relearning how to approach food preparation, and her considerable creativity in developing low carb recipes. We hope you enjoy our efforts.

CHAPTER 2

Understanding the Low Carb Mechanism

"Obesity is always accompanied by insulin resistance ..."
Dr. Peter J. D'Adamo

The Backdrop of Confusion

Anyone in our society who has ever considered changing their eating habits, whether to lose weight or for better health, has a right to be confused. If you have ever had an opportunity to watch a television program hosting a panel of 'experts' on dieting, you are almost guaranteed to be confused. There is so much information available today that it is virtually impossible to sort the 'wheat from the chaff'. Even if you devote an extraordinary amount of effort to wade through the information, you need more than a general knowledge of nutrition, anatomy and physiology to make sense of it all. This is a daunting task that most individuals will not, or cannot, complete. Peoples' thirst for knowledge that will help them is reflected in the number of publications devoted to the subject. Dr. Walter Willett, a nutritional epidemiologist at Harvard Medical School, states that a new diet or nutrition book hits the bookshelves every other day. During our research for this book Patricia visited a large bookstore and identified 35 titles on the shelf dealing with some aspect of low carb eating.

This backdrop of confusion is one of the reasons we decided to write our book. It is important for you to know from the outset that this is not a scientific textbook. This chapter has not been written with the expectation that it would satisfy the scientific reader. It is simply a basic explanation that the ordinary person concerned about their weight or their health, can read and understand. Since you are at least considering adopting a low carb lifestyle (why else would you be reading this book?), it is important for you to understand why low carb living is healthy. It is equally important to understand the mechanism that makes weight loss, and weight control, so much easier than you have ever before experienced or even imagined.

We said this wasn't going to be a scientific book, and it is not. That doesn't mean the information didn't come from scientific sources, because it does. We will frequently refer to those sources and give credit where appropriate. Our task has been to translate that information into text and ideas that are easy to understand. Join us on a journey of discovery and learning.

How Low Carb Works

The body is basically a complicated energy converter. It acquires energy in the form of fuel from food and drink, and converts it into another form, energy that runs all bodily functions, from digesting food to running marathons. There are only three types of food energy available to the body. They are carbohydrates, fats and proteins. We all know about fats. For as long as most of us can remember we have been urged by medical and nutritional experts to avoid fat at all costs. Carbohydrates have been accepted, even promoted, as the mainstay of our diet if we want to stay healthy. It turns out our experts have been wrong on both counts. Fats aren't bad, at least not *all* bad. And carbohydrates aren't all good, at least not in the quantities we have become accustomed to eating.

When the energy converter (the body) receives a load of fuel (food) it has to choose which type of fuel to burn first – carbohydrate, fat or protein. The body will always follow the path of least resistance and burn whatever is easiest to convert. The fuel that is easiest to burn is carbohydrate. You know this from your own experience. You can probably remember being involved in an activity, like walking or playing ball, and finding yourself in need of some quick energy. If you are like most North Americans you ate a chocolate bar, a bag of chips, or drank a Coke. In each case the fuel you consumed was pure carbohydrate. Why did it give you quick energy to continue your activity? Because that is what carbohydrates do. They are easily converted by the body into immediately available energy in the form of sugar. At this point we experience a blood sugar high. As soon as the ingested carbohydrate has been converted to sugar in the blood a natural control mechanism kicks into gear. The pancreas is stimulated to release a surge of insulin to force the sugar (glucose) into muscle, liver and fat cells where it can be used for immediate energy, stored so it is readily accessible for energy or placed in long term storage (as fat).

What has happened to our society over the last two or three generations is that the proportion of our food that is carbohydrate has increased substantially. In order to digest this high load of carbohydrate our body has become accustomed to releasing relatively large amounts of insulin. Here is the normal sequence of events. You eat your high carbohydrate meal consisting of some dinner rolls with your appetizer, a baked potato, some carrots and peas, a nice piece of chocolate cake for dessert, and a teaspoon of sugar in your tea. Does this sound like anything you might have eaten lately? You probably had a piece of meat, or chicken or fish with your potatoes and veggies, but it doesn't come into this equation because it is protein, not carbohydrate. We have just loaded you up with a high carbohydrate meal.

What is your control mechanism going to do? The pancreas is going to release insulin, and lots of it. The message the controller (pancreas) got was 'Big load coming down'. The insulin does its job, in fact overdoes the job, because the controller couldn't be precise in terms of how much carbohydrate was in the 'big load' and released more insulin than was necessary. The result is the insulin pushes more sugar into the muscle, liver and fat cells than would be ideal. Now you have a low blood sugar. How does that make you feel? It might make you feel a little sluggish, lethargic, or even sleepy. Have you ever had that mid afternoon low after a nice (high carbohydrate) lunch? It is likely that you also felt hungry at this point. This is a defense mechanism to boost your blood sugar again.

Let's summarize the sequence of events. When you eat a high carbohydrate meal the body immediately converts it to sugar and you experience a blood sugar high. The body releases insulin, probably too much, pushing the sugar from the blood to the muscle, liver and fat cells causing you to have a blood sugar low. You get drowsy – and hungry. That is the other consequence of the low blood sugar, it causes you to feel hungry. What do you do when you get hungry? Why, you eat more carbohydrates.

The long term effect of this cycle of too much carbohydrate followed by too much insulin is that the body becomes less responsive to the action of insulin. This condition is called 'insulin resistance'. This unresponsiveness causes the pancreas to put out even more insulin to try to get the job done. The state of having the insulin level more or less permanently high is called 'hyperinsulinism'. There are two common medical conditions (they often go together) that are apt to result from this vicious cycle. The high demand on the pancreas to produce insulin may 'wear out' the pancreas and cause diabetes. Secondly, because the insulin is not being effective in converting the blood glucose into energy, it stores more and more of it as fat, which results in obesity. Studies have shown that obese and diabetic individuals are often extremely unresponsive to the action of insulin.

Your reading may bring you in contact with a subject referred to as 'Syndrome X'. A brief description of this topic will help you understand how it fits with the discussion about insulin. First it is useful for you to know that the medical community refers to a 'syndrome' when there are a group of medical conditions that seem to come together but there isn't an explanation as to why. Syndrome X is a cluster of medical conditions, known as metabolic disorders, which include insulin resistance, obesity, blood fat abnormalities, glucose intolerance (diabetes) and high blood pressure. Syndrome X doesn't mean all of these conditions are always present, but some of them often occur together.

A Special Word About Diabetics

You probably know someone, or know of someone, who has diabetes. You may have some appreciation that the problem in diabetes is that the body cannot produce enough insulin. What is the result? The carbohydrates that have been converted to sugar cannot be adequately moved into the cells and the body ends up with too much carbohydrate, in the form of sugar, in the blood. If left uncontrolled, there may be serious consequences for the diabetic. You may also know that the diabetic is equally at risk of getting too much insulin, either because too much was injected, or because the diabetic didn't consume enough carbohydrate for the insulin that was injected. This imbalance between too much insulin and too little carbohydrate can lead to diabetic coma. So what impact does low carb living have on diabetics? Eating fewer carbohydrates requires less demand for insulin thus the diabetic will usually find that once established on a low carb diet, they can decrease the amount of insulin they must inject. This is exactly what happened to our friend John, and he wasn't even officially on a low carb diet. His wife Annette had adopted low carb eating to lose weight so he was experiencing some changes in his diet as well. Within a very short time his blood sugar levels revealed that he needed less insulin.

How Did So Many of Us Get So Fat?

The harmful effects of eating carbohydrates that are rapidly converted to blood sugar are implicated in both heart disease and diabetes. These harmful effects are especially serious for people who are overweight. (Willett, *"Eat, Drink, and Be Healthy"*, p.19) You may have thought that being overweight was the result of eating too much. For a long time we have been taught to believe that weight control is simply a matter of: calories in equals calories out. This implies if we balance the number of calories we take in, with the number we expend in our activities, our weight will be controlled. Then why are so many people in our society fat? And we are fat. More than one in every two people in North America is overweight. One in every five is obese (obesity is usually considered to be more than 20% above ideal body weight) (Willett, p.56). Drs. Michael and Mary Eades, *"The Protein Power Lifeplan"*, believe the situation is even worse: "… 74 percent of adult Americans are overweight *to some degree*." (p.32) You probably fit into one of these groups or you wouldn't be reading this book. The statistics are alarming, not because overweight people are concerned about their body image, but because of the health risks involved. These risks include, but are not limited to, heart disease, Type II diabetes, stroke, high blood pressure and high cholesterol.

How *did* so many of us get so fat? You might think it's because we ate too many calories, and too much fat. It certainly is possible to eat too many calories as a contributor to being overweight. And fat can make up a lot of those calories, but these are not the principle 20th century villains. The more recently identified culprit is our carbohydrate intake and the hyperinsulinism it causes. This isn't because insulin is bad, but because of what our diets force insulin to do. As we ingest our high carbohydrate diets (the late 20th century curse) we produce high levels of sugar in the blood, as described earlier. The insulin charges forth to move the sugar into the muscle cells, or store it in the liver for later use. If the storage cells are full, the insulin will convert the excess to a fatty tissue called triglyceride. That is a main constituent in adipose tissue – plain old body fat! (Atkins, *"Dr. Atkins' New Diet Revolution"*, p. 50) When we consume an excess of carbohydrates we force insulin to store that excess as fat. *The reason so many of us are fat is because our diets are too high in carbohydrates.*

Harmful Effects of High Carbohydrate Diets

It seems logical that if we reduce the amount of carbohydrate in our diet we will lose weight, or find it much easier to maintain our weight. That is exactly what low carb living is all about. The choice to live 'low carb' also has some healthy side benefits. Remember insulin and its constant conversion of extra blood sugar into fat? High insulin levels have many other unhealthy effects of which we need to be aware. (Atkins, p.54) The following list is not exhaustive.

- ♦ Insulin increases salt and water retention, both of which contribute to high blood pressure and being overweight.
- ♦ Insulin makes the arteries more responsive to adrenaline thereby aggravating high blood pressure.
- ♦ Insulin can cause or complicate sleep disorders.
- ♦ Insulin is directly involved in creating hardening of the arteries.
- ♦ Insulin is a contributor to high levels of triglycerides, blood fats involved in hardening of the arteries.
- ♦ Insulin is a contributor to high levels of 'bad' LDL cholesterol.
- ♦ Insulin is a contributor to low levels of 'good' HDL cholesterol.

It is important to remember that insulin isn't really bad. The hormone must deal with the excesses we choose when we eat. It is even more important to remember that if we eliminate those excesses we will reduce, or eliminate, the negative effects produced by insulin.

The Fat Story

Elsewhere in this book we provide considerable guidance on how to eat low carbohydrate. Some of the meal plans and recipes may include increasing the amount of fat you currently consume. For many of you this will be a frightening prospect because our information over the past three decades has been that 'fat is bad'. We want to reassure you that such a simple perspective is just flat out wrong. Dr. Walter Willett of the Harvard School of Medicine, in his book *"Eat, Drink, and Be Healthy"* has done a wonderful job of putting the fat story in perspective. We cannot portray it more clearly than he does so we are going to use his words. Dr. Willett (p.56) said: "… we have lost sight of the critical fact that not all fats are the same. Or, to put it more bluntly, not all fats are bad. In spite of the scorn heaped upon dietary fat and the antifat recommendations from the country's leading health organizations, the truth is that **some fats are good for you, and it is important to include these fats in your diet.** In fact, eating more good fats – and staying away from bad ones – is second only to weight control on the list of healthy nutritional strategies." So the strategy for you, and for us, must be to make sure most of the fats we ingest are the good ones. That is what the recommendations in our book will help you do.

The 'fat' family is very complex. Understanding it is difficult, so we have chosen to model our discussion after Dr. Willett (p.61) to provide you with the practical relationships between the 'good' and 'bad' fats and your health. There are four main categories of fat that we eat – saturated, monounsaturated, polyunsaturated, and trans fatty acids. What you need to understand in order to eat healthy is which are the good ones, which are bad, and where do we find each type.

The 'good' fats are the unsaturated ones, either monounsaturated or polyunsaturated. They are usually in liquid form. We find the monounsaturated fats in olives and olive oil, canola oil, peanut oil, cashews, almonds, peanuts, most other nuts, peanut butter and avocados. We find the polyunsaturated fats in corn, soybean, safflower, and cottonseed oils and fish. These are the 'good' fats that you should be increasing in your diet. It is important for you to know that there is a group of 'good' polyunsaturated fats known medically as 'essential fats'. This is because the only way the body can get these fats is from our diet. These essential fats are needed for building cell membranes, making sheaths that protect nerves, making hormones and chemicals that control blood clotting, and for muscle contraction. (Willett, p.62)

The 'bad' fats are the saturated fats and the trans fatty acids. Saturated fats are found in high quantities in whole milk, butter, cheese, ice cream, red meat, chocolate, coconuts, coconut milk and coconut oil. The trans fatty acids are found in most margarines, vegetable shortening, partially hydrogenated vegetable oil, deep fried chips, many fast foods, and most commercial baked goods.

This is a whole lot of information that may be hard to remember at first. You will find it necessary to refer back to this information periodically *as you start reading the labels in grocery stores*. In order to make low carb living *easy*, it will be necessary for you to have a conscious awareness of which are the healthy choices, including which foods to choose to ensure you get 'good' fats.

Although you may have a vague idea that fat is related to heart disease, you probably don't know just how the problems develop. That lack of knowledge isn't important to your health as long as you know there is a link and what you can do to avoid it. What you need to know to minimize the risk of heart disease is that *it is beneficial to increase your intake of* 'good' *fats and decrease your intake of* 'bad' *fats*. If you accomplish that, these are some of the benefits you will achieve:

- ♦ Lower levels of low-density lipoprotein (LDL), the 'bad' cholesterol.
- ♦ Higher levels of high-density lipoprotein (HDL), the 'good' cholesterol.
- ♦ Prevention of the increase in triglycerides that results from high carbohydrate intake.
- ♦ Reduction of the development of erratic heartbeats, the main cause of cardiac death.
- ♦ Reduction of the tendency for blood clots to form in arteries.

If you compare these benefits with those achieved by decreasing your carbohydrate intake discussed earlier, you will realize that three simple steps: lowered carbohydrate usage, decreased 'bad' fat consumption and increased 'good' fat intake, combine to produce many health benefits.

What is most encouraging is that if you follow these three simple steps, you will gain all those health benefits while you also lose weight. Or, if weight loss is not a goal, you will find it easier than ever to maintain your weight. Maintaining a healthy weight is a significant health benefit. As Dr. Willett says (p.35), "… next to whether you smoke, the number that stares up at you from the bathroom scale is the most important measure of your future health." Harv's personal opinion as a physician is that maintaining normal weight is more important to health than any of the other individual benefits we have discussed. Being able to take advantage of all the benefits is ideal.

Healthy Eating Guidelines

If you have ever searched for 'official' guidelines to healthy eating you have probably accepted Canada's Food Guide, or the U.S. Department of Agriculture (USDA) Food Guide Pyramid, as reliable sources. We have some bad news. Both of those guides are outdated. Neither guideline is based on the scientific knowledge now available to us. On the other hand, perhaps that is good news. We can expect that adoption of the practices outlined earlier, following new scientific knowledge, will deliver health benefits which have eluded us until now.

There is a new kid on the 'Food Guide' block that is based on current science and research results. It is the 'Healthy Eating Pyramid' (figure 1) developed by Dr. Walter Willett of Harvard Medical School. The fundamental difference between Dr. Willett's pyramid and the advice in the previous guides is the place of carbohydrates and good fats. The older guides considered ALL fats to be bad and thus recommended their use only sparingly. The Healthy Eating Pyramid (HEP) puts 'good' fats at the base of the Pyramid, to be consumed at virtually every meal. Previous guides placed carbohydrates such as bread, cereal, rice and pasta at the base of the pyramid, to constitute 6 to 11 servings per day. The Healthy Eating Pyramid places those foods at the top of the Pyramid, to be used sparingly. Furthermore, Dr. Willett's Pyramid considers potatoes and sweets in the same category as bread, cereal, rice and pasta, to be consumed sparingly. Simply put, Dr. Willett has turned the pyramid upside down. The advice and guidance available to you in our book follows the principles laid out in Dr. Willett's Healthy Eating Pyramid.

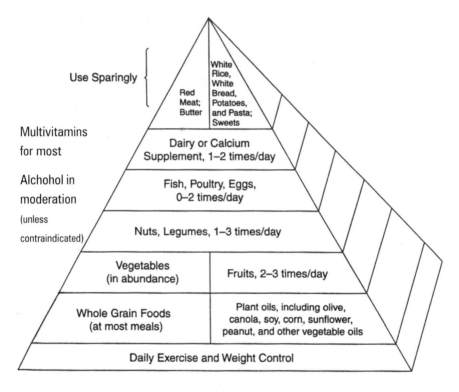

Fig 1. Willett's Healthy Eating Pyramid

Glycemic Index and Glycemic Load

Recent research has identified a wide variation in the rate at which carbohydrates release their sugar into the blood. Some carbohydrates make blood sugar in a flash, others much more slowly. Researchers at the University of Toronto have developed a means of classifying foods according to how quickly they are broken down into sugar and absorbed into the bloodstream. This rating system is called the 'glycemic index', or GI. Why is this important? You will remember that carbohydrates generally cause a rapid increase in blood sugar, stimulating a rapid release of insulin. Those foods with a high GI release the sugar so quickly that the ensuing insulin release is at its most damaging. The alternative, choosing foods that have a low GI, results in a more sustained absorption into the bloodstream therefore avoiding the sudden insulin high. If you make the effort to become familiar with the glycemic index of your favorite foods, you can make wiser decisions about which are most healthy for you. As a general rule of thumb, foods low in carbohydrates will have a low glycemic index.

Following the development of the glycemic index, researchers identified an even more accurate system of guiding your selection of the healthy carbohydrates. This latest system is known as the 'glycemic load'. This classification is based on multiplying the amount of carbohydrate (number of grams) in a *normal serving* of a food by the glycemic index (grams of carb x glycemic index = glycemic load). Dr. Willett (p.93) gives a couple of examples that really help to understand the difference between a high and low glycemic load. "A carrot, then, with a high glycemic index value of 131 and 4 grams of carbohydrate *(normal serving size)*, would have a glycemic load of about 5 (131%=1.31 multiplied by 4 equals 5). In contrast, a cup of cooked pasta, which has a glycemic index of 71 and 40 grams of carbohydrate *(normal serving size)*, provides a glycemic load of 28." It is evident from these examples that the glycemic load of carrots is very low compared with that of pasta. This method is complicated, and to be completely accurate it has to be calculated in a clinical setting. That level of accuracy isn't essential if we just want to have an indication of which carbohydrates to choose. In the back of this book we have included a 'Carb Counter' to provide you an easy reference for the number of grams of carbohydrate (*in a normal serving*) of many common foods. You may wish to seek out a glycemic index scale so you can calculate the glycemic load of your favorite foods. Familiarity with the glycemic load of a food enables you to choose items that have the least insulin stimulating effect.

Effective Carbohydrate Content

Drs. Michael and Mary Dan Eades, in their book *"The Protein Power Lifeplan"*, present the concept of 'Effective Carbohydrate Content (ECC)'. (p.323) Their theory is that fiber, though it is a carbohydrate, is structured in such a complex way that the body's digestive system cannot break it down into sugar and absorb it into the blood. This means fiber does not stimulate the release of insulin and therefore does not contribute to the negative health effects we associate with high carbohydrate intake. Drs. Eades recommend the fiber portion of our food not be counted as carbohydrate in our daily calculation. This refinement in the way you count your carbs can make a significant difference with some foods. However, it does make your 'carb counting' more complicated. We don't find it necessary to calculate the fiber in our carbs, but if you wish to take full advantage of your selected daily carbohydrate intake, you may wish to investigate this option further.

Eating Low Carb

As previously mentioned, in order to eat 'low carb' it will be necessary to become familiar with which foods are high in carbohydrate content. You may also wish to become knowledgeable about glycemic index and carbs with high glycemic load. This isn't as ominous as it sounds. Right off the bat you know that foods such as bread, cereal, rice, pasta, potatoes and sweets are high in carbohydrate and will have to be consumed sparingly. What do we mean by 'sparingly'? We mean consuming only as many grams of carbohydrate per day as are required to maintain your 'ideal' weight. For most of us that will be somewhere in the range of 50 to 100 grams per day. The daily intake for maintenance will vary for each of us, depending on our metabolism and activity level. It will require some trial and error for you to determine exactly how many grams of carbohydrate you can consume without either gaining or losing weight. If you are heavier than your 'ideal' weight you will have to consume less than 50 grams per day, more likely about 30 grams, during your weight loss phase. How much less will depend in part on the rate of metabolism of your body and in part by how quickly you wish to lose the weight. We find that for most people a carb intake of 30 grams per day will provide an acceptable rate of weight loss.

Apart from this Chapter and the next, this book is devoted to providing guidance you can follow for *easy low carb living*. It is important to remember, as you travel this new road to healthy living, that there are no absolutes. Once you determine the number of grams of carbohydrate you can eat each day to maintain your weight, or how many you are going to consume during weight loss, it is up to you *which* carbohydrates you choose. Of course you will refer to the 'Easy Carbohydrate Counter' in Chapter 12 to assist you in making healthy choices. However, once you have completed your weight loss, if you occasionally want to splurge, because you have a burning desire for a dish of ice cream for example, then do it! Be aware that every ½ cup will have 16 – 20 grams of carbohydrate. This means that if you are targeting 60 grams per day to maintain your weight, the ice cream will constitute one third of your allowance for the day. That doesn't mean you can't have the ice cream, but it does mean you will have a challenge in modifying your intake for the rest of the day to stay under the 60 grams total.

You might want to consider making your choice based on volume of food rather than taste. For example, you could eat a large salad, or coleslaw and two cups of vegetables, or some fruit, to make up the 20 grams of carbohydrate. Whichever you choose you will have consumed a major portion of your daily allowance. That is fine, simply decrease your carbohydrates for the remainder of the day, to adhere to your target. Remember you have control. These are *your healthy eating* choices. You decide which foods are included in the guidelines you are following.

Eating the Right Fats

The other half of the healthy eating equation is to ensure you increase your consumption of the 'good' fats and minimize the 'bad' ones. That isn't quite as simple as choosing foods that are low in carbohydrate, but it is certainly possible with a little effort. You probably already know that red meats, especially fatty red meats, are high in 'bad' saturated fats, so eat red meat infrequently. When you do choose to include red meats, make sure they are lean cuts. Get in the habit of choosing fish, pork or poultry instead. None of these foods have significant quantities of saturated fats.

The other bad fats are the trans fatty acids. These are probably the most difficult to reduce or eliminate from your diet unless you are eating low carb, in which case it follows quite naturally. Many of the fast foods North Americans consume, especially those that are deep fried, are cooked in these fats. French fries for example, hit you with a triple whammy of negative health effects. First, potatoes are high in carbohydrate content, having 35 grams in every 4 ounces of potato. Second, they have a high glycemic index of 95 so the glycemic load is 33. To make matters worse, when cooked as french fries they are usually deep fried in oil containing trans fatty acids. So how important are french fries in your diet? We don't eat them and we don't recommend them.

If you are a pastry lover you need to know that a large proportion of commercially prepared pastries are also cooked with oils containing trans fatty acids. Most pastries are also very high in carbohydrates. The last group of food products that have a high content of trans fatty acids are margarines. Not all margarines contain these bad fats, so you will need to read labels and avoid those identified as being hydrogenated or partially hydrogenated. It is the hydrogenation process that generates the trans fatty acids in margarines. That same negative effect will be present in any hydrogenated cooking oils. Make it a habit to read labels before you buy. After all this bad news, the good news is that you can decrease, or eliminate, most of the trans fatty acids in your diet by avoiding deep fried fast foods, pastries, and some margarines.

Vitamin Supplements

No doubt you will have heard controversy about the use of vitamin supplements. Most traditional nutrition advisors will maintain that if you follow the recommendations in the 'Food Guide' you don't need supplements. That thinking is outdated in our view. It does not take into account the loss in nutrient value in our foods resulting from chemically stimulated growth, early harvest to accommodate lengthy distances of transport to market, the time of the transport, storage time in warehouses and on stores shelves, and the delay between purchase and use. If the food is frozen it loses additional nutrients. Each step in that process takes some nutrient value out of the food.

So even if you manage to eat all the types and amounts of food recommended, you are likely to be short of the required nutrients. The stark reality is that in our modern lives of rushing from here to there, we seldom manage to get the right balance of food. Add the possibility that some of the nutrient value may not get absorbed because of medication you are taking, temporary ill health, or alcohol consumption, and there is a very high likelihood that your body isn't getting all of the nutrients it needs for maximum health.

The logical way to make up our shortfalls is to add the missing nutrients in the form of supplements. Dietary supplementation is increasingly accepted, and even recommended, by dieticians, family doctors and academics. What should you take? The answer to that question is specific to your individual circumstances including age, gender, diet and health status. For those who consider themselves to be in good health, with a reasonably healthy diet, we recommend a standard store brand multivitamin, multimineral supplement plus an additional 400 mg capsule of Vitamin E be taken daily. If you are not in full health, you ought to seek medical counsel for a prescription that specifically fits your needs.

Understanding the low carb mechanism makes us aware that we have tremendous potential to control our health. If we reduce our carbohydrates, decrease our intake of bad fats, increase our consumption of good fats, and add the insurance of vitamin supplements, we will feel better and be healthier. We will also either lose weight or maintain our ideal weight more easily. The choice is ours.

CHAPTER 3

Understanding the Low Carb Revolution!

"In the last decade, we Americans have cut our intake of fat
from 38 to 34 percent of our daily calories, and yet
we've each put on an average of eight pounds."
Suzanne Somers

This chapter is devoted to providing a brief explanation of many of the popular diet books in the market today. We will present an overview of the basic principles underlying each diet. We intend to leave you with an understanding of these principles that will allow you to make informed choices. You may notice that even though each diet takes a slightly different approach representing the individual interpretation of the author, the underlying scientific basis remains the same for all. It is not our intention to convince you that one diet is better than the other, although we express our own opinion about the merits of various approaches. In the end this is still *your healthy eating* program. The choice must be yours.

Eat, Drink, and Be Healthy, Walter C. Willett, M.D.

This isn't really a diet book, yet we choose to review it first. Why? Because in our opinion it represents the best 'summary of the science' available. Just as important, it is written in lay person's language, making it an easy to understand source of information. So much of what is presented in the market is based on opinion and anecdotal information that it is difficult to know what to believe. Dr. Willett is Chairman of the Harvard School of Public Health and a Professor of Medicine at Harvard Medical School. He is a world-renowned researcher, considered by many to be the pre-eminent nutritional epidemiologist in the world today. We believe we can trust the science behind the information he provides.

The way Dr. Willett presents his information is extremely useful to a lay reader. He uses the introduction to set the stage and then devotes a chapter to each major nutritional issue. A scan of the chapter titles provides a picture of the scope of his work.

Introduction
What Can You Believe About Diet?
Healthy Weight
Surprising News About Fat
Carbohydrates for Better and Worse
Choose Healthier Sources of Protein
Eat Plenty of Fruits and Vegetables
You Are What You Drink
Calcium: No Emergency
Take a Multivitamin for Insurance

He completes each chapter with a section called "PUTTING IT INTO PRACTICE". This helpful section makes it easy for the reader to apply the information that has been presented.

The basic concept that Dr. Willett presents is revolutionary. It sets the nutrition world on its' ear because he argues, based on the available science, that the existing US Department of Agriculture (USDA) Food Guide Pyramid (Fig. 2) is *wrong*. He uses research results to support his argument to literally turn the pyramid upside down. Instead of bread, cereal, rice, and pasta being the base of the pyramid with 6 - 11 servings per day, his 'Healthy Eating Pyramid' (Fig 3) puts them at the top of the pyramid, to be used sparingly. He also removes potatoes from the vegetable group and treats them as another food to be used sparingly. Dr. Willett says this new way of eating is a "… strategy aimed at improving your health instead of a diet aimed solely at helping you shed pounds."(p.17) We think this is really important, and that is why our book approaches *Easy Low Carb Living* as a healthy eating option, not just a weight loss opportunity.

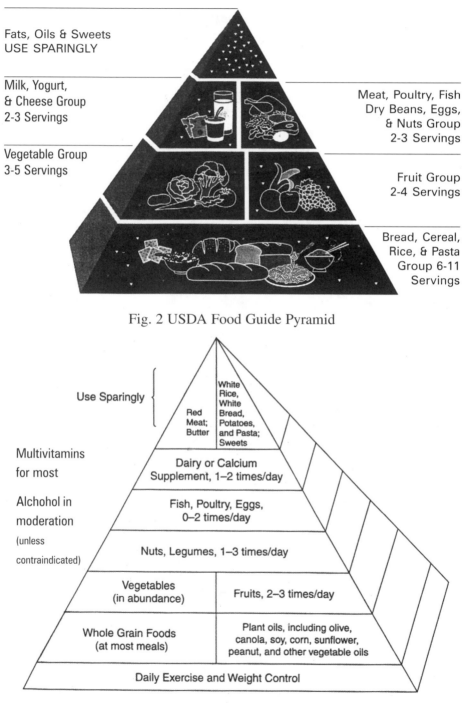

Fats, Oils & Sweets
USE SPARINGLY

Milk, Yogurt,
& Cheese Group
2-3 Servings

Meat, Poultry, Fish
Dry Beans, Eggs,
& Nuts Group
2-3 Servings

Vegetable Group
3-5 Servings

Fruit Group
2-4 Servings

Bread, Cereal,
Rice, & Pasta
Group 6-11
Servings

Fig. 2 USDA Food Guide Pyramid

Use Sparingly

Red
Meat;
Butter

White
Rice,
White
Bread,
Potatoes,
and Pasta;
Sweets

Multivitamins
for most

Dairy or Calcium
Supplement, 1–2 times/day

Alchohol in
moderation
(unless
contraindicated)

Fish, Poultry, Eggs,
0–2 times/day

Nuts, Legumes, 1–3 times/day

Vegetables
(in abundance)

Fruits, 2–3 times/day

Whole Grain Foods
(at most meals)

Plant oils, including olive,
canola, soy, corn, sunflower,
peanut, and other vegetable oils

Daily Exercise and Weight Control

Fig. 3 Willett's Healthy Eating Pyramid

Dr. Willett offers his opinion regarding the seven healthiest changes you can make in your diet (p.22-24):

1. Watch your weight.
   In his words (p.35): "… next to whether you smoke, the number that stares up at you from the bathroom scale is the most important measure of your future health."
2. Eat fewer 'bad' fats and more 'good' fats.
   As we discussed in the previous chapter, the challenge is to decrease the 'bad' saturated fats found mostly in red meats and dairy products and the trans fatty acids found in hydrogenated oils and margarines. The beneficial side of the fat equation is to increase the unsaturated fats found in oils like olive, corn, soybean, sunflower, peanut and canola.
3. Eat fewer refined-grain carbohydrates and more whole-grain carbohydrates.
   Quickly digested (and high carbohydrate) foods like white bread, white rice, pasta, potatoes and sugars need to be decreased and multi grain breads, rice and whole grain pasta used instead.
4. Choose healthier sources of proteins.
   Use red meats only sparingly and choose beans, nuts, fish, poultry, and eggs to provide healthier sources of protein.
5. Eat plenty of vegetables and fruits, but hold the potatoes.
   Plentiful use of vegetables and fruits is an essential part of any healthy diet but Dr. Willett's position is that potatoes ought to be excluded from this category and treated strictly as a source of carbohydrate with minimal nutritional value.
6. Use alcohol in moderation.
   One drink of alcohol a day for women, and one or two for men, has been shown to have a health benefit, except for those individuals for whom addiction is a risk.
7. Take a multivitamin for insurance.
   Vitamin supplementation won't replace what is missing in an unhealthy diet but it will replace vitamins missing in the diet of even the most conscientious eater.

There are three basic steps to weight control according to Dr. Willett (p.48):

1. Physical activity.
    This is a critical component of weight loss and we have included a separate section in Chapter 4, encompassing Dr. Willett's recommendations.
2. Find a diet that works for you.
    The strategies in Dr. Willett's book are a good place to start for any individual. Our book, *Easy Low Carb Living,* also provides extensive practical guidance for how to lose weight and maintain the weight loss.
3. Become a defensive eater.
    Most of the suggestions offered by Dr. Willett are incorporated in our book.

Dr. Willett's book will be useful for anyone interested in learning more about nutrition in general. It is written in easy language that we all can understand. This book represents the best 'summary of the science', in our opinion.

Dr. Atkins' New Diet Revolution, Robert C. Atkins, M.D.

This is only one of several books that Dr. Atkins has in print. He is undoubtedly the best known and most published of all proponents of the low carb approach to diet. His work and opinions have come under much criticism over the years but as research 'catches up' it appears that Dr. Atkins may have been ahead of his time. Most of what he has advocated for years is becoming more accepted within mainstream medicine.

Dr. Atkins' experience is that if people follow his guidance they can achieve and maintain weight loss safely. He has over 25 years of clinical practice in this field so he is intimately familiar with how different individuals react to low carbohydrate dieting. Dr. Atkins' extensive experience has prompted him to provide advice in his book for even complicated cases. Those who experience serious resistance to weight loss, or who have significant medical problems, ought to be under the care of a medical professional with expertise treating weight loss by low carb dieting. Those who are basically healthy (but overweight) can follow Dr. Atkins' written guidance relatively easily, and safely.

Dr. Atkins sets out what he calls "the facts" at the beginning of his book. What he has to say provides a good overview of the 'overweight' issue and puts the context of his book in perspective. Rather than paraphrase him, we have chosen to quote 'his facts' for you. (p.5-6)

1. "Almost all obesity exists for metabolic reasons. Most studies have shown that the obese gain weight on *fewer* calories than people without a weight problem.

2. The basis of the metabolic disturbance in obesity has been pretty well worked out by the scientists over the last ten to fifteen years. It doesn't have to do with the metabolism of the fat you eat but with hyperinsulinism and insulin resistance. The insulin hormone and its effect on your blood sugar levels (which are constantly rising and falling in response to the food you eat) is far more directly related to your general health picture and to your likelihood of being victimized by killers such as heart disease and stroke than was ever suspected in the past. It is also *the single most important determinant of your weight*. That is why, by the fifth decade of our lives, 85% of Type II diabetics are obese.

3. This metabolic defect involving insulin can be circumvented by restricting carbohydrates. When you restrict it, *you avoid the food subdivision that causes you to be fat*.

4. This metabolic correction is so striking that many of you will be able to *lose weight* eating a *higher* number of calories than you have been eating on diets top-heavy in carbohydrates. The so-called "calorie theory" has been a millstone around the necks of dieters and a miserable and malign influence on their efforts to lose.

5. Diets high in carbohydrates are precisely what most overweight people don't need and can't become slim on.

6. A carbohydrate-*restricted* diet is so effective at dissolving adipose tissue that it can create fat loss *greater* than occurs in fasting.

7. Our epidemics of diabetes, heart disease, and high blood pressure are very largely the products of the hyperinsulinism connection.

8. The Atkins diet can correct and has corrected these serious medical complications of obesity. Indeed, 35% of my patients come to me for help with cardiovascular problems. The Atkins diet is probably the most aggressively health-promoting diet you will ever have the opportunity to be on."

The basis of Dr. Atkins' plan is that dramatic restriction of carbohydrate intake will cause the body to enter a condition he calls Benign Dietary Ketosis (BDK). In order to get into BDK it is necessary to reduce carbohydrates to below 40 grams per day. This is difficult, given that most people in our North American society consume somewhere in the order of 300 grams per day. Being in 'ketosis' simply means that your body is burning your fat stores as a source of fuel. It is the reduced availability of sugar (sucrose) through the decreased carbohydrates that forces the body into ketosis.

There are many health benefits to the reduced carbohydrate level, as we have discussed in the previous chapter. A major benefit to those seeking weight control is the appetite suppression that accompanies carbohydrate reduction. Furthermore, the higher proportion of fat in the diet as a result of the decreased carbohydrates provides increased satiation. The combination of suppressed appetite and an increased feeling of satiation is very helpful to anyone trying to lose weight. For you the dieter, the first thing you will notice is that you aren't hungry. The second thing you notice is that you have more energy. These benefits will occur on any low carb program.

There are three aspects of Dr. Atkins' program about which you should be concerned. First, he advocates that when someone starts on his weight loss program they should reduce their carbs to 20 grams or less a day. This is a *very* low level of carbohydrate intake. We believe that most people can achieve successful weight loss at 30 grams without the extreme changes that are associated with 20 grams or less. Second, his advice for vitamin supplementation is extremely complex and though we have no basis to criticize, we find it more difficult than most people will be able to follow without medical help. Third, his guidance for what products will meet your needs most conveniently promotes his own product line. There is nothing inherently wrong with that so long as you are aware it is simply an option. You can follow an effective and healthy low carb lifestyle with foods readily available in your local market.

This is an important book for anyone interested in knowing in more detail how the low carb mechanism works. It is useful to read the information from the 'guru' himself.

Live Right For Your Type, **Dr. Peter J. D'Adamo**

This is a fascinating book, but much too complicated for the average person seeking guidance in how to eat healthy for weight loss and maintenance. Our experience is that the vast majority of people are looking for guidance that is healthy and easy. Indeed, that is what motivated us to write *Easy Low Carb Living*. For those who are interested in a detailed set of guidelines as to how to live a healthy lifestyle, or those who are struggling with chronic illness, Dr. D'Adamo's book may useful.

His basic thesis is that our blood type (O, A, B, or AB) and whether we are what he calls "secretors" or "non-secretors" determines for each of us how our bodies behave. It is his opinion that it is our 'type' that establishes what kind of personality we have, our response to stress, our emotional stability, how we digest our food, the way the metabolism works in our body, our immunity, and what toxicity we experience. He provides detailed and complicated guidance regarding how to make each aspect of our life as healthy as possible.

Of most interest to us are his Dietary Guidelines. What he recommends for those who are Blood Type O or B is consistent with the guidance we provide here in *Easy Low Carb Living*. Anyone choosing to adopt his recommended lifestyle could follow the low carb living program we offer, to meet his Dietary Guidelines. For those who are Blood Type A or AB, it is a little more complicated. Our guidance will still work, but to follow his guidelines will require you choose more soy and fish for your protein sources and reduce significantly the use of chicken or red meat.

The testimonials that Dr. D'Adamo provides are very similar to the stories we hear all the time from people who have chosen to adopt a low carb lifestyle. This is especially true with respect to the effects of decreasing or eliminating wheat, potatoes and pasta.

This is the second book regarding diet and blood type by this author. Anyone who is interested in learning more about this approach will want to read both books.

The Carbohydrate Addict's Diet, Dr. Rachael F. Heller and Dr. Richard F. Heller

This very popular diet book provides guidance on the basis that each of us has more or less of a predisposition for being addicted to carbohydrates. The authors have developed a test to determine whether an individual has a: 1) Doubtful Addiction; 2) Mild Carbohydrate Addiction; 3) Moderate Carbohydrate Addiction; or 4) Severe Carbohydrate Addiction. Their contention is that if you test positive for addiction you ought to follow their Carbohydrate Addict's Diet.

The theory of their diet is that there are two factors at play for the carbohydrate addict: the *frequency* at which carbohydrates are eaten, i.e., how many times a day, and the *duration* during which they are consumed, i.e., how much time is spent in the consumption process. The Hellers' claim is that if 'addicts' consume their daily carbohydrate load at one sitting (called a "Reward Meal") in less than an hour, they will avoid the hyperinsulinism that is ostensibly the root cause. They say it doesn't appear to require a reduction in the amount of carbohydrate consumed at that one sitting. For the other meals in the day, they recommend keeping fiber high and fat and carbohydrates very low.

We have no judgement to make as to whether carbohydrate addiction is manifest as the Heller work maintains. Indeed, if anyone accepts their tenet, tests positive and wishes to undertake their recommended diet plan we see no reason to discourage them. We would however, recommend that the total daily carbohydrate intake be kept low for all the health reasons we have recommended elsewhere in our book. What this would require is choosing to follow the Heller recommendation of eating high fiber and low fat and carbohydrate during the day and then eating nearly all of the daily allowance of carbohydrates at one meal in a time of less than an hour. We believe the total level of carbohydrates should be restricted for health reasons in spite of the Hellers' suggestion that carbs can be consumed in large quantities so long as it is done at the Reward Meal, in less than an hour and in 'balance' with fiber, proteins and fats.

This book has been very popular. The ideas expressed are intriguing, and the test for carbohydrate addiction is interesting to take. We have serious reservations about the 'Reward Meals' recommended by the authors. Anyone who feels that they may be addicted to carbohydrates will want to read this book.

The Protein Power Lifeplan, **Dr. Michael R. Eades and Dr. Mary Dan Eades**

This is a low carbohydrate, high protein diet plan for weight loss. The authors review the lack of success of the low fat approach to weight loss. They explain that, "Clearly the low-fat diet hasn't been the panacea that many had hoped for; in fact, it has turned out to be a dismal failure, a fact admitted publicly in 1996 by most of the world's experts in nutritional research." (p. xix) If it has been admitted publicly that the low fat approach to weight control is a dismal failure, why has this fact taken so long to filter down to the general public, and to many family doctors?

The authors suggest that carbohydrates are virtually the only foods that cause people to 'binge'. They believe that this is so because carbohydrates activate a reward center in our brains that overrides common sense and any feelings of being full. They explain that, "…just the thought of carbohydrates overrides your brain signals telling you that you're full. Carbohydrates fail to trigger our off switch." (p.17) There is considerable discussion of the insulin mechanism, and hyperinsulinemia. They review the medical impacts that are likely a result of any diet high in carbohydrates. There is an extensive section on various medical conditions, and the possible positive impact upon these conditions of reducing our carbohydrate consumption.

These authors suggest that we can get all the nutrients we need without eating any grains or potatoes. They make the point that many of the nutrients we need are fat-soluble nutrients that actually need small amounts of fat in order for the body to absorb them. They suggest that many of the cancer fighting nutrients, such as antioxidants, cannot be well absorbed by the body unless they are eaten with small amounts of fat. They recommend that green salad always be eaten with a dressing made of extra virgin olive oil, or canola oil, to ensure the absorption of these nutrients. They also recommend that we drizzle olive oil or butter on any steamed vegetables.

One of the interesting hypotheses suggested by these authors, is that our stomachs and digestive tract were not designed to deal with grains and grain products. They suggest that our ancestors (the hunter-gatherers) were healthier because they ate only meat, vegetables, fruits and nuts.

There is a lot of science in this book, but it is not so difficult that the average reader will have trouble understanding it. The authors go to considerable trouble to explain the insulin connection, how cholesterol impacts our health, all about antioxidants and their use, and how diet impacts the autoimmune system. The authors review issues related to fructose, the simple sugar found in fruit, and its absorption into the blood stream. They talk about the proliferation of products on the market that use fructose as the sweetening agent. While the quantities of fructose found in honey and fruits is relatively small, the amount added to commercially prepared foods is considerable. They blame the rise of diabetes and obesity in North America on this fact.

Although there is a lot of good information in this book, we disagree with some of the recommendations. For example, the authors caution against the use of sun block. They suggest we spend time building up a tolerance to the sun so we can tolerate longer periods without burning our skin. They suggest we do this to facilitate the production of vitamin D and melanin. This recommendation is in direct conflict with our knowledge of the damaging effects of the sun and the risk of skin cancer.

The authors present an overall plan for health that deals not only with diet, but also includes recommendations regarding exercise, rest, stretching your mind, meditation and relaxation. As with other programs, Drs. Eades suggest that this is a program that should be adopted as a 'lifeplan' and not a program that is suitable if used on a short term basis.

One of the ideas put forth by these authors with respect to carbohydrates, is that the fiber in a carbohydrate will impact the amount of carbohydrate that is absorbed by the body. Essentially, they say that raw fiber is not absorbed or broken down by the digestive system and therefore has no effect on the insulin mechanism. They have developed a formula to demonstrate this theory where they call the carbohydrate left over after we take out the fiber, the 'Effective Carbohydrate Content (ECC)'. The formula is:

"Total Carbohydrate - Dietary Fiber = Effective Carbohydrate" (p.323)

To use this formula in calculating your daily carbohydrate allowance, you will of course need to know the dietary fiber in the carbohydrates. The authors list the major low carbohydrate vegetables and fruits and provide some guidance with respect to the fiber content and its impact on daily consumption. Using this rule of thumb impacts how we view carrots. They become a vegetable that can be eaten on a low carb diet, especially if eaten raw. These authors have published another book that contains a carbohydrate gram counter that includes the fiber content and the ECC of most foods.

This is another very popular low carb diet. We know of many people who have followed the diet recommendations outlined in this book with considerable success. It is a more difficult read than other books. To implement their plan most effectively, a reader will want to purchase both of their books so they have a means to determine the ECC of foods.

The X Factor Diet, Leslie Kenton

The author of this book is unique among the authors of the diet books we have reviewed. She is a journalist and brings to her writing an ease with words that fosters an understanding of difficult concepts that scientists don't often achieve. It is fortunate that she is able to do so because she covers a large amount of historical and scientific information. Her tracking of the historical changes in eating patterns is a compelling way to convince us of the importance of the move back to low carb eating. She also conveys the impact the agricultural revolution had on changing our eating habits. Ms. Kenton's coverage of these topics is very useful to any reader seeking to understand the background to present dietary patterns.

Ms. Kenton takes the name of her book from 'Syndrome X', a constellation of conditions associated with insulin resistance. She has developed a diet program with two components, Ketogenics and Insulin Balance. Ketogenics is a diet designed for those individuals who are significantly overweight, which she defines as more than 35% of body weight as fat in females, and more than 22% in males. She suggests that the Ketogenic program will significantly decrease the fat level, overcome insulin resistance, increase metabolic rate, decrease sugar cravings, eliminate constant hunger, detoxify the body and increase energy levels. The Insulin Balance program is designed for those individuals who range from normal weight to moderately overweight. She claims that this program will decrease fat levels, stave off aging, increase lean body mass to fat ratio, detoxify the body and increase energy levels. The main differences between the two programs are that the Ketogenic program places greater emphasis on foods that have carbohydrates with a low glycemic index, has a higher protein content in the diet, and includes omega 3 fatty acids.

The author presents a detailed argument for the health benefits of whey protein. She particularly identifies the importance of buying microfiltered whey protein concentrates or whey peptide blends, since other products will not have retained the essential molecular structure necessary to be effective in the body. We agree with Ms. Kenton that it is an excellent source of convenient protein.

Ms. Kenton tries hard to make her comprehensive presentation of this very complex subject easy to understand. We think she has succeeded in making the background material understandable but her diet programs are not simple. In part this is because she is advocating a total change in eating patterns to gain maximum health benefit. Her intention is commendable but it is our feeling that most readers will be a little overwhelmed. She does salvage her attempt at simplicity to some extent by providing a 27 page section called the "The X Factor Diet Idiots' Guide".

This is a good book for anyone wishing to get an understanding of the history of how our western society has transformed itself into one of high carbohydrate consumers. It is also a useful book for the reader who wants to adopt a diet that offers maximum health benefit. We have no doubt the diet will work, but those who choose to follow it have to be prepared to be serious students of the programs.

The Zone, Barry Sears, Ph.D.

This is a book that promotes a type of dietary regime that is essentially low carb but 'with a twist'. The author is a biochemist. He has a particular interest in diet, biochemistry and heart disease. He has spent considerable time unraveling the secrets of how the body utilizes food, and what happens at a cellular level when we metabolize food. Although there is some scientific jargon in this book, it is well written and reasonably easy to understand.

The diet promoted in this volume is one that will transport its followers into that elusive state of peak performance known in sports as 'The Zone.' The author contends that this diet will enhance physical performance, sharpen mental acuity and optimize health. There is an actual formula for the diet, which allows the application to be specific to each individual. He explains, "You must eat food in a controlled fashion and in the proper proportions ... The dietary technology required to reach the Zone is as precise as any computer technology. The rules of this dietary technology may appear complicated at first, but I think once you put them into practice you'll find they're exceptionally easy to follow." (p.3) This is a technically difficult book in some parts. The determination of your individual protein requirement is complicated.

There is some very good discussion about carbohydrates and how they contribute to the storage of excess fat in our bodies. The author provides explanations of the insulin mechanism, the glycemic index of foods and other contributing factors to the fattening of the North American population. There are lengthy scientific explanations of other mechanisms within the body that contribute to fat storage, and various disease states. Some of the science was totally new to us, such as the descriptions of good and bad "eicosanoids" and their impact on our health. The author has made an effort to describe some of these mechanisms in terms that are easy to understand.

There are many interesting anecdotes about athletes with whom the author has tested his approach to diet. It would appear that elite athletes do get a boost from eating what the author calls a "Zone-favorable" diet. The author has also tested this diet on ordinary individuals, and persons suffering from a variety of chronic and other diseases. His contention is that the dietary principles applied in reaching the Zone will help the body fight a variety of disease states. The author contends that following a Zone-favorable diet will have positive effects on heart disease, arthritis, diabetes, blood pressure, and even cancer. (Of course, many of these conditions are equally responsive to a low carb plan.) The anecdotal evidence is compelling. The author recommends his approach to diet for everyone, to optimize their health, improve mental status and enhance physical performance. This book was not written, nor was this diet developed, primarily for weight loss. Weight loss is a side effect of the diet, if the participant was overweight and eating a high carb diet prior to starting this approach.

The formula necessary to determine your diet to reach the Zone is based on your individual protein needs. The Zone diet allocates a defined proportion of your daily food intake to carbohydrate and fat, in certain proportion to your protein requirements. Your individual protein requirements are determined by a set of calculations involving your lean body mass (your weight and your percentage of body fat) and your activity level. All the calculations can be accomplished using the tools provided in his book.

We found this a fascinating read. There is a lot of science in this book, some of it quite complicated to wade through. The calculations necessary to develop individual protein requirements are a complicating factor in trying to adopt this approach. This book is appropriate for anyone who is interested in athletics and enhancing physical performance.

Eat Great, Lose Weight, Suzanne Somers

This is a book that has enjoyed considerable popularity. Ms. Somers is a well-known and extremely attractive woman. We are not surprised at the popularity of a publication that holds out the promise we can all look like her.

Ms. Somers has developed an approach to weight loss and weight maintenance based on her own personal experience and the theories concerning 'food combining'. *"Fit For Life"* is another book that promotes food combining as a weight loss method, and we will review it later in this chapter. The theory behind food combining is that different types of food, for example protein versus carbohydrates, need a different environment to be properly digested. The proponents of this approach suggest that the stomach juices needed to digest meat are different from the stomach juices needed to digest carbohydrates. If we eat both types of food together, they contend that we do not properly digest either food and the result of this is indigestion, flatulence and weight gain. Ms. Somers suggests that eating proteins and carbohydrates together strains the digestive system.

Another important concept in food combining is that fruits must always be eaten alone – never in combination with any other foods. The reason given is there is too much natural sugar in fruits, and they lose their nutritional value if eaten with anything else. (The authors of the other food combining book have a slightly different theory on this subject.) If you want to eat fruit while following this method, you can do so first thing in the morning, then wait 30 to 90 minutes before eating anything else. If you have had a meal, you are advised to wait 2 to 3 hours before eating any fruit.

In her book, Ms. Somers promotes a diet plan using what she calls Level One (for weight loss) and Level Two (for maintenance.) Using Level One requires that you eliminate from your diet a group of foods she labels "funky foods" because they "wreak havoc" on the digestive system. The foods that need to be eliminated include sugar, refined carbohydrates, caffeine and alcohol. Ms. Somers then divides the rest of the allowable foods into four groups called 1) Proteins & Fats 2) Veggies 3) Carbos and 4) Fruits. Once you have sorted this out, there is a fairly detailed series of rules about eating and combining these food groups. For example, you may eat protein and fats with vegetables, or carbos with vegetables, but no fat. You must never combine proteins with carbos.

In Level Two you are allowed to add back small quantities of the "funky foods" that were eliminated in Level One. The basic rules of food combining remain unchanged. You never eat fruit with anything else using this approach to weight control. Although Ms. Somers provides recipes that include sugar (in reduced quantities) and flour, she readily admits that, "In general, I find that the fewer carbs I eat, the more weight I lose." (p. 43) She does allow what she refers to as "carbo" meals, like a pasta meal, but never in combination with any protein, or fats.

Ms. Somers' approach is not a strictly low carb approach, and it is not a strict food combining approach to eating. While this combination has proved both effective and successful for her, we believe that it overcomplicates the issues. We are both somewhat skeptical about the theories and practice of food combining. We believe that it would take a considerable amount of time and effort to adjust to eating foods only in the combinations that are recommended by this approach. It also seems to require major changes in eating habits, and some inconvenience to eat fruits in isolation, for example. We are told that there are many people who are happy to follow this approach, and who 'swear' by it.

The book does provide a fascinating glimpse into the life of a famous personality, including family photos and little personal vignettes. Anyone interested in her life, or in the application of food combining principles to everyday life, may want to read this book.

Fit For Life, Harvey and Marilyn Diamond

This is the other book that promotes food combining as a weight control mechanism. The book goes into detail concerning the theories and practice of food combining. The approach is somewhat more scientific than the approach taken by Suzanne Somers. These authors follow a concept called 'natural hygiene'. Harvey Diamond studied natural hygiene for over ten years, receiving a doctorate in nutritional science from the American College of Health Science in Austin, Texas. He suggests that this is an approach that will have wide spread health benefits, if followed correctly.

This book details three natural body cycles, and suggests ways to eat that will enhance the body's ability to deal with each of these cycles. The cycles are "on a daily basis we take in food (appropriation), we absorb and use some of that food (assimilation) and we get rid of what we don't use (elimination)." (p.26) The author further delineates the normal hours during which each of these cycles takes place. He suggests the following schedule:

"noon to 8 pm   appropriation (eating and digesting)
8 pm to 4 am   assimilation (utilizing the nutrients from the food we have eaten)
4 am to noon   elimination (you know what this is)" (p.27)

Did you notice in the schedule that the appropriation or eating phase only starts at noon? That's correct, this method suggests that you eat nothing but fresh fruit and fruit juices until noon – ever! As with the Somers method of food combining, you never eat fruit except on its own. These authors suggest that fruit passes very quickly through the stomach and into the intestines where it is easily absorbed by the body. They state that this is the most important aspect of their program and that eating only fruit or fruit juices until noon is the most important change you can make for your health. They propose that because fruit has such a high water content, it requires less energy than other foods to be digested. They provide actual timetables to determine how long you must wait after eating other foods, before you are allowed to eat fruit.

Both authors are vegetarian, and would like to convince the reader that the consumption of 'flesh' is not necessary for health. They advocate eating the majority of vegetables raw, rather than cooked or processed in any way, in order to get the most out of the nutrients. The authors present a formula or ladder of foods to be consumed, in order to maximize energy. At the bottom of the ladder are fruits and fruit juices, next we have fresh vegetable salads and fresh vegetable juices (lunch), then we graduate to steamed vegetables, with raw nuts and seeds, then to grains, breads, potatoes and legumes, and finally to meat, chicken, fish and dairy. They claim that the highest energy levels will be achieved on days that only fruits and vegetables are consumed.

Marilyn Diamond is a nutritionist who has developed a number of recipes to complement the approach to food that is recommended by her partner. All of the recipes are presented as part of a full four week menu plan to get you started on the correct path. This approach to eating is recommended as a life time commitment to good health and weight control. As with the Suzanne Somers approach, it is not suggested as a short term solution to either health problems or weight control.

In general we find that even though these authors try to put science behind their argument, we remain unconvinced, as in the case of Suzanne Somers. We find the idea of eating only fruit until noon to be a difficult one to contemplate. We think the food combining approach complicates life and makes it much more difficult to continue to function within the constraints of normal everyday living. Again, we have met people who swear by this approach to eating and are willing to organize their lives around the principles set out in this book.

Anyone who is interested in learning in more detail about the theory and practice of food combining will be interested in this book.

The False Fat Diet, **Elson M. Haas, M.D.**

This is a book based on the premise that extra fat, especially around the middle of the body, is "false fat" as a result of an allergic type reaction to various foods. This theory is based on the idea of how our individuality and metabolism can impact our ability to digest certain foods. Dr. Haas has an extensive history of treating patients for obesity and other physical ailments, by determining their food sensitivities and eliminating the foods that cause reactions. A reaction to a food may be as simple as indigestion or as complicated as a skin rash or a headache. This book offers a methodology to help anyone sort out whether they are reacting to certain foods.

The author postulates that the reactions to foods that we are sensitive to contribute to what he calls "false fat" in the following ways:

"1. Food reactions cause fluid to surround invading food particles.

2. Food reactions release hormones that cause fluid retention.

3. Food reactions make intestinal membranes swell.

4. Food reactions disrupt cell chemistry, causing fluid storage.

5. Food reactions cause capillaries to leak fluids.

6. Food reactions cause gas production." (p.50)

One of the concepts in this book is that while we consume foods we may be reacting to, we are also causing the immune system to work overtime trying to deal with the body's reactions to these foods. The author postulates that if we eliminate these reactive foods from our diet, the immune system is strengthened and better able to cope with other issues such as hay fever or arthritis. It is suggested that if you suffer from hay fever and are regularly eating foods that you are sensitive to, you may unwittingly be exacerbating your symptoms. If you eliminate the reactive foods from your diet the reaction to hay fever might disappear, as the immune system is freed up to cope more effectively with pollens in the air.

The author lists seven foods that are most often the cause of reactions. These foods are dairy products, wheat, sugar, soy, peanuts, corn and eggs. He recommends an elimination diet to help the reader determine if they react to any of these foods. He outlines a series of increasingly restrictive diets to determine your level of reaction to certain foods. You then reintroduce the seven sensitive foods, one at a time, to isolate your body's response. Dr. Haas makes the point that many of the processed foods we consume today are full of chemicals, additives, and fillers. Processed foods also contain high quantities of the sensitive foods to which people react. His solution is to determine your sensitivities, and eliminate these foods from your diet altogether. He recommends we eat unprocessed whole foods such as fresh fruit and vegetables, fish, poultry, nuts, rice and other whole non-reactive foods.

The book provides a food reaction reference guide and some interesting recipes. The author explains that food reactions can create metabolic roadblocks to weight loss by:

- ♦ "Slowing the metabolic rate,
- ♦ Increasing the hormones that cause weight gain,
- ♦ Creating hypoglycemia,
- ♦ Depressing energy, and
- ♦ Contributing to illness." (p.63)

This is a program that recognizes the failure of the low fat approach to diets. Dr. Haas recognizes a type of individual who is best suited to eating animal protein to help stabilize their energy supply. In many ways it supports the idea of a low carb approach to eating. Dr. Haas says that, "Ironically, many people who have tried hard to eat wisely have become hypoglycemic, because they are eating too many carbohydrates and not enough protein. People who live on carbohydrates – mostly fruits, grains, and starchy vegetables – become hypoglycemic more easily than people who have a more balanced diet, with higher amounts of protein." (p.65) Dr. Haas says that of all the food cravings, "carbohydrate craving is the most common." (p.61)

The book includes a chapter that provides considerable detail concerning the medical conditions Dr. Haas believes may be caused by food reactions. Dr. Haas provides some menu planning and other prescriptives for healthy living, including the need for exercise and the need to regulate our response to stress.

This book makes a lot of sense in many ways and is an interesting read. Anyone who thinks they may have food sensitivities will want to read this volume.

CHAPTER 4

Easy Low Carb Lifestyles

"The human body is healthiest on a low carb diet."
Leslie Kenton

What Is A Low Carb Lifestyle?

Do you want to be healthier? Have more energy? Lose some weight? Maintain your current weight? Deal with other health concerns? All this is possible by adopting a low carb lifestyle. A low carbohydrate lifestyle means limiting your carbohydrates. It does not mean eliminating your carbohydrates. This would be virtually impossible to do as almost all foods contain carbohydrates. Furthermore, a diet without any carbohydrates would be unhealthy. Proteins and fats do not contain carbohydrates. Vegetables, fruits, grains, nuts and seeds all contain carbohydrates. We will teach you to recognize those foods that have lower carbohydrate content than others, and how to change your eating habits to take advantage of this knowledge.

A low carbohydrate program for weight loss is designed to help you lose weight by burning fat, rather than sugar, for energy. How strictly you adhere to the low carbohydrate plan will determine the amount of weight lost. In most cases low carbohydrate eating will result in increased energy and a sense of general well being, in addition to weight loss (or weight maintenance if that is your goal).

In general, as discussed in the previous chapters, our bodies produce the energy we need by burning either sugar or fats and proteins. What happens on a low carbohydrate weight loss plan is you dramatically reduce the carbohydrates you eat, and force the body to burn fat for energy. The real trick is to eat less fat than you need for your daily routine to start the body burning stored fat. This mechanism results in weight loss. The low carbohydrate plan that we use is not 'protein-loaded' like some of the popular diets. There is some suggestion that protein loading (larger than normal portions of protein in lieu of carbohydrates) may cause calcium to leach from the bones. This is not a side effect that is healthy for anyone, but particularly for women. The plan we follow has normal portions of protein, with reduced carbohydrates. It has lots of vegetables and salads, and fruit is allowed in small portions during weight loss, and in larger portions in the maintenance period. Our program also includes an increase in the 'good' fats.

Paradigm Shift

Perhaps the single most difficult part of starting a low carb approach to food is the shift in thinking that is necessary. It requires what we refer to as a paradigm shift – that is, a dramatically different way of viewing the world of food and diet. For years, those of us who are health (or weight) conscious, have tried to cut down our fat intake. This, we were told, would improve our health, allow us to lose weight and forestall heart disease. Current research has shown this approach has not achieved the desired results. While the production and consumption of 'low fat' foods have proliferated, we have continued to get more and more over-weight as a group. There has not been a noticeable improvement in the incidence of heart disease. The earlier review of Dr. Willett's research emphasizes that a departure from this way of thinking is necessary. The research supports reduction of carbohydrates as a method to help lose weight and control blood sugar. There may be other possible health benefits resulting from this approach to eating, depending on your current status and metabolism.

The paradigm shift is most difficult for the person responsible for food planning, shopping and preparation. After years of searching out 'low fat' products and learning the low fat method of preparing foods, you now must switch your thinking to low carb. If you are buying salad dressing for example, you will want to avoid the low fat variety and buy the regular dressing. Manufacturers need to add something to their low fat products to increase flavor. They usually replace the fat with sugar! This makes low fat salad dressings much higher in carbs than the normal variety.

Thinking about food from a new perspective can be difficult initially. We need to learn which are the low carb foods we can consume without problems. We need to adjust our thinking to low carb rather than low fat. We don't want to suggest that we don't care about the fat in our diet – we do. But we have learned that it is much more important what type of fat is being consumed as far as health is concerned. We have also learned that if you count (and control) the carbs in your daily food intake the rest generally looks after itself.

> *"I have been trying the recipes in Everyday Low Carb Cooking and Bert and I are finding them very tasty. I am not a good cook and never experimented with spices. Bert just didn't like to try anything different, he has sure changed... tells me 'you can try this again'."*
> Donna Mueller, Victoria, British Columbia, Canada

General Low Carb Approach

The basic outline of the low carbohydrate plan that we follow is contained on the following pages. The plan entails no more bread, cereals, potatoes, rice, pasta or sugar during weight loss, with slightly more flexibility during maintenance. Fruit is allowed in small portions during weight loss and increasing portions during maintenance. It is easier to follow than you might think. This approach to eating is simple, flexible and portable. There is no weighing, measuring, calculating points or counting calories. You can easily adapt your meal plans to include eating out in restaurants, at friends homes, or enjoying a guilt free and healthy vacation.

You will need to learn to count your carbohydrate intake. This will enable you to track your consumption in an organized manner. We have provided some tools to facilitate this in later chapters. You will find a simple food diary (Chapter 11) with suggestions on how to keep it up to date, and a basic carbohydrate counter (Chapter 12) so that you can make informed decisions about what you eat. The most difficult part about a low carbohydrate meal plan is that it is not particularly intuitive, especially at the beginning.

We think this is because we have been so conditioned to worry about low fat foods, or to count calories, that we have not learned much about carbohydrates and sugar. We certainly didn't realize the negative impact sugar can have on our health and our weight. Once you learn some of the basic values of foods, in terms of their carbohydrate content, it becomes easier and more intuitive with respect to what you will want to eat.

Keeping a daily journal of the foods you eat, and in particular the grams of carbohydrate, will allow you to track your successes and identify the reasons for any set backs. The purpose of a food diary is to demonstrate from day to day and week to week where you have made good decisions, and identify areas that need to change. Our food diary provides space each day to chronicle exercise and make any special notes. This allows you to readily recall your activity level and any special circumstances or activities that might impact your day. For example, Patricia had a small piece of store bought Birthday Cake on our grandson's birthday. He was thrilled that his Nana would eat something that she normally doesn't, to celebrate his special day. Patricia noted "Dean's Birthday Cake" in her diary, to help her recall why her carb count was so elevated on that particular day. It is important to note that one small piece of cake did *not* impact Patricia's weight. She paid particular attention to her carb intake for the balance of the week, and saw no change when she weighed herself at the end of the week. This is managing her carb intake and being flexible, without any negative side effects.

Weigh yourself only once a week. We do faithfully, every Sunday morning. People who have been dieting for years sometimes develop a negative reaction to weighing themselves. If you really don't want to get on a scale, that is your prerogative. If you stick to the low carb approach you will soon notice changes in how your clothes fit and how you feel. A concern if you decide not to record your weight, is that you will not have an accurate record of your results. It will be more difficult for you to determine if there are foods that have caused a small increase, or whether you are losing or maintaining your weight. The choice is obviously yours to make. We do not recommend stepping on the scale everyday. There are too many fluctuations from day to day that can be caused by other agents, not just weight loss. The issues of fluid retention and hormonal changes can significantly effect weight. Weighing on a daily basis may also cause us to fixate on the scale, rather than on the process in which we are engaged.

We still record our weight, each week. In fact, we have developed graphs that illustrate weight against our daily average carbohydrate intake, over time. We use it as a reference tool only. It does not make us panic or despair if small fluctuations occur. We expect that to happen. Keeping an accurate record enables us to analyze why these fluctuations occur, and then make better decisions in the future. Some of these fluctuations are actually unintended additional weight loss. Patricia, in particular, is prone to losing an extra pound or two in a week if she is too busy. It is not that she *ever* forgets to eat, but simply that her level of activity in a very hectic week will burn an unusually high amount of fat and so an additional pound or two will drop off. Patricia does not want to lose any more weight, so she makes an effort to eat some extra carbs the following week (often in the form of fruit or desserts) to gain back that pound or two.

Average North American Diet

Before discussing the low carbohydrate approach to food, it may be worth reflecting on the typical North American diet. Calculate your carbohydrate intake for a week, before starting a low carb approach to eating. Using the carb counter we have provided in Chapter 12 will help you do this. In many cases, you may be surprised at the high carb content of your current diet. We are not trained in school to think of breads and potatoes as turning to sugar in our bodies, but that is exactly what happens. We have provided a sample daily diet to demonstrate this fact.

		Carbs
Breakfast	orange juice	29
	raisin bran cereal, sugar, ½ cup of skim milk	60
	coffee with cream	0.5
10:00 a.m.	carrot muffin	30
	coffee with cream	0.5

Noon	turkey sandwich	49
	potato chips	19
	soft drink	42
3:00 p.m.	granola bar	35
	soft drink	38
Dinner	grilled chicken breast	0
	baked potato with butter	51
	carrots	8
	dinner roll with butter	14
	2 chocolate chip cookies	52
	tea	0
9:00 p.m.	2 cookies	52
	tea	0
Total carbohydrate intake		**480**

Weight Loss Plan

The basic formula is very simple. To lose weight you should keep carbohydrates to fewer than 30 grams a day. You may lose up to 5 pounds during your first week on this plan, especially if you follow it closely. Some of this weight loss will be fluid loss. You can generally expect to lose 1.5 to 2.5 pounds a week following this plan. Each of you will experience the weight loss according to your particular metabolism. While Patricia averaged 2.5 pounds every week while she was following a weight loss regime, Harv can easily average between 4 to 6 pounds of weight loss in a week. Harv exercises more vigorously than Patricia does, and we attribute his increased rate of weight loss to the effect this exercise has on his metabolism.

Everyone has a slightly different metabolism. You will be able to adjust the recommended carbohydrate intakes to accommodate your metabolism and the amount of exercise you perform. During weight loss keep your carbohydrate consumption to less than 30 grams a day. This is easier to do than you might think. The chapter on menu planning provides a full week of menus for weight loss. These menus do not exceed 30 grams of carb on any day. They include 3 meals and 2 snacks every day.

It is interesting to note that Patricia has had readers write to her after using her cookbook, to say they were unable to consistently maintain 30 grams of carb or less on a daily basis. Many of these readers were able to lose weight by maintaining 40 grams of carb on a daily basis. Much depends on your individual metabolism, and how dramatic a change in your carb intake you have made, compared with your previous eating habits. Only you can determine what is best for you. Some of the popular low carb diets recommend an even more dramatic reduction in carbohydrates for the first week or two to initiate weight loss.

It will take a period of trial and error to determine exactly how much or how little carbohydrate you can tolerate, and still lose weight. Tracking your intake and your weight in a food diary will help you determine your threshold.

Our experience, and the experience of many of our readers from the cookbook, is that a reduction to 30 (or even 40) grams of carb a day will result in weight loss. We want this to be a pleasant experience for you, not a punishing one. There is a lot to learn to shift your life long eating habits. A program that allows 30 grams of carbohydrate a day will provide you with sufficient flexibility and variety that you will not find it an arduous task. We would like you to consider that this approach to eating is one that you *can* use for the balance of your life. At 30 grams of carbohydrate a day you will see dramatic results within a very short period (probably 10 to 14 days). The results will not be limited to weight loss, but will extend to increases in your energy level and general feelings of well being. If you reduce your carbohydrate intake to 40 grams a day, instead of the recommended 30 grams a day, your weight loss will be somewhat slower. You will still lose weight but it will be more gradual.

We provide a method to help you determine what level of intake is most appropriate for you in Chapter 6 on Strategies For Success. Changing eating habits that have taken years to develop will not be easy. Results will not appear overnight. You will have some days that are more difficult. On our weight loss regime, there is no such thing as 'cheating'. You make daily choices concerning how closely you want to stick to your plan. (We hate the connotations associated with the word cheating. It implies dishonesty. We suggest that you take the word out of your vocabulary and instead talk about choosing to be 'strict' or 'not-so-strict' with your carb intake.) Eating higher carb foods on a daily basis will cause your weight loss to slow down or even stall. Depending on the number of carbs you have consumed, you may even see a weight gain. The number of carbs you consume will determine the fluctuations in weight, both up and down. Once you start a low carb approach you will quickly see what we mean. It is a very powerful tool and usually provides immediate feedback to reinforce your decision.

We would like to caution you here, not to try to lose the weight too quickly. If you are like us, you probably put on the extra pounds over a period of years. If this is the case, it doesn't make sense to try to take it all off within a couple of weeks. You will probably see a fairly dramatic weight loss in the first week of a low carb approach. You may lose anywhere from 5 to 10 pounds when your system initially switches to burning fat for energy rather than sugar. Once the system adjusts to this switch in metabolism, the weight loss will slow to anywhere from 1.5 to 2.5 pounds per week. This slightly slower rate will be healthier for you and easier for your body to accommodate. This method will allow you to eat well, not feel hungry or deprived, and continue a slow and steady loss. At 2.5 pounds a week, you will lose 10 pounds a month! It doesn't take very many months on this plan before you will have lost a significant amount of weight.

"As I grew up, I was always tall and thin and 'NEVER' had to watch what I ate. Then I turned 35 and everything started to change. In the year 2001, I celebrated my 40th Birthday and was overweight and felt uncomfortable about it, but didn't really know what to do about my situation. I had lunch with Harv and he told me all about Patricia's cookbook project. I was excited and asked him many questions about it. We agreed to get together in a couple of months when Patricia would be travelling with him.
The most motivating force that allowed me to change my way of eating was meeting Patricia and Harv for lunch last summer. Patricia looked fabulous and I felt chubby and overweight. I was excited to listen to Patricia and hear her success story in her quest to lose weight - before she celebrated her milestone birthday. She was enthusiastic about her 'new image' and made it sound so easy to achieve if only one put one's mind to the task."
Sheila Bernardi, Calgary, Alberta, Canada

We have provided a sample meal plan for a typical day on the weight loss plan. This outline does not reflect specific recipes, but takes a generic approach to demonstrate what sort of foods you can expect on an average day. Eat 3 good meals and 2 or 3 snacks everyday during the weight loss period. Because you will be consuming foods that have lower carbohydrate content, they will not cause blood sugar highs and the corresponding drops in blood sugar that previously may have made you feel hungry, sleepy or even irritable a few hours after eating. Eat until you feel pleasantly full and satisfied. You should not have that 'stuffed' feeling that is typical after a high carbohydrate meal.

On this meal plan you should not feel 'starving' between meals. It is normal to feel hungry before we eat. It is also normal to feel some initial hunger while following the weight loss plan. If you feel hungry when you get up from eating a meal, then you are not eating enough. Add green salads and other low carb vegetables to help satisfy your hunger. The hunger should gradually abate as your system adjusts to metabolizing low carbohydrate foods. Your blood sugar will be more constant as these foods are absorbed, and the pancreas is not required to produce as much insulin. We have included a basic count of the carbohydrates for illustrative purposes and we have kept the menu similar to the average North American daily menu used earlier.

Weight Loss - Sample Daily Meal Plan

		Carbs
Breakfast	glass of water	0
	2 scrambled eggs	1.2
	2 strips of bacon	0
	coffee with cream	0.5
9:00 a.m.	glass of water	0
10:00 a.m.	½ low carb bar	1
	decaff coffee with cream	0.5
Noon	turkey salad (not a sandwich)	8.5
	coleslaw	4.0
	glass of water	0
	herb tea	0
3:00 p.m.	1 celery stick, 1 tablespoon cream cheese	.8
	Fresca*	0

Time	Item	Carbs
5:00 p.m.	glass of water	0
Dinner	broiled chicken breast	0
	steamed cauliflower	2.5
	steamed asparagus	3.8
	green salad	3.0
	glass of water	0
	sugar free jello	0
	herb tea	0
8:00 p.m.	glass of water	0
9:00 p.m.	sugar free jello (if desired)	0
	herb tea	0
10:00 p.m.	glass of water	0
Total carbohydrate intake		**26.8**

* This drink contains aspartame.

Maintenance Program

Do you want to maintain your current weight? Do you want to keep off the weight you lost using the weight loss plan? It is simply a matter of increasing your carbohydrate intake. It is an easy and flexible approach to weight maintenance. You don't dramatically change the foods you have been eating, you just increase the carbohydrate consumption in an average day. You choose which carbs you want to eat to effect this increase. To maintain your ideal weight, carbohydrate intake may vary from 40 or 50 grams a day, to as many as 90 to 100 grams a day depending on your metabolism and your activity level. Start your maintenance program with a carbohydrate content of approximately 45 grams a day. After two weeks at this level, if you are continuing to lose weight, you should increase your carbohydrate consumption another 5 to 10 grams a day and review again in a week. This will allow you to determine what level of increase is best for you in order to maintain your ideal weight.

Daily carbohydrate intake for maintenance can vary widely, depending on your individual metabolism and your lifestyle. Harv can eat close to 100 grams of carb a day and not put on any weight. Of course, he runs 6 miles, four times a week. This constitutes a large expenditure of energy and allows him to burn off the extra carbs that he consumes without any gain in weight. His level of fitness also ensures he has a high metabolic rate. Patricia generally keeps her carb intake to between 50 and 60 grams a day without any weight gain. This too is slightly higher than recommended in most of the popular low carb diets. Patricia also exercises by walking – at least 30 to 45 minutes of brisk walking every other day is her normal routine. This exercise, plus her normal metabolism, allows her to eat at this level without any weight gain.

Remember, controlling your carbohydrates will allow you to eat well without any real hunger and without gaining back any of the weight that you worked so hard to lose. A low carb approach is unlike other diets in that this is not a short term approach that needs to be dramatically changed when the ideal weight is gained. There are no pre-packaged foods. The portion control is not so severe that you experience a yo-yo effect when you stop 'dieting'. You should not go back to your former method of eating, but instead increase your carbohydrate intake by increasing your consumption of fruits or eating larger quantities of other low carb foods. Your 'old' (pre low carb) diet is probably what contributed to your weight gain in the first place. We think that you will feel so well while on a low carb plan that you will not want to go back to your old habits.

With the low carb approach to maintenance you still control your carbohydrate intake but you are able to dramatically increase this intake without weight gain. This means you can choose to increase your fruits, or add a delicious dessert now and then. You may even choose to have some whole grain bread or whole grain pasta (if wheat is not a sensitive food for you). We will show you how to make the choices that will enable you to increase the variety and level of carbs without any detrimental effects on weight or other health issues. We have tried to keep the sample daily meal plan for maintenance similar to the samples used earlier in this chapter.

Low Carb Maintenance - Sample Daily Meal Plan

		Carbs
Breakfast	glass of water	0
	Magic Muffin***	7.8
	coffee with cream	0.5
9:00 a.m.	glass of water	0
10:00 a.m.	½ Citrus Low Carb Bar***	2.7
	decaff coffee with cream	0.5
Noon	Mushroom & Spinach Frittata**	3.6
	green salad	3.0
	glass of water	0
	herb tea	0
3:00 p.m.	8-10 almonds	3.5
	Fresca*	0
5:00 p.m.	glass of water	0
Dinner	roast chicken breast	0
	Creamy Garlic Cauliflower**	3.5
	Grilled Zucchini**	3.4
	Greens with Pecans & Blue Cheese**	5.9
	glass of water	0
	French Cream**	4.0
	herb tea	0
8:00 p.m.	glass of water	0
9:00 p.m.	sugar free jello (if desired)	0
	herb tea	0
10:00	glass of water	0

Total carbohydrate intake   **38.4**

* This drink contains aspartame.
**Recipes designated with ** are found in Patricia's cookbook, *Easy Low Carb Cooking*.
*** Recipes designated with *** are found in Chapter 8, New & Amazing Recipes.

General Health Benefits

Patricia's experience with low carbohydrate eating is in many ways very typical. She started eating a modified low carb diet to lose weight and was successful in that endeavor. She noticed an almost immediate increase in her energy level and wondered if it would continue if she maintained a low carb approach to foods. (It has!) Perhaps the most dramatic change, however, was the impact it had on a health problem that Patricia has had since she was 18 years old. Patricia has a bowel disease called colitis. This condition has resulted in years of trying to deal with uncomfortable symptoms on a daily basis. The severity of the symptoms would ebb and flow, but they were always present. Since changing her diet to a low carb approach the symptoms of this disease have completely disappeared.

In consultation with her specialist, we now assume that Patricia has a 'sensitivity' to wheat. When Patricia eats wheat products they aggravate her condition and increase her symptoms. Within 10 days of starting to eat low carb, Patricia announced that she had no intention of ever going back to her old ways. It has been over two years since she made this decision, and it is reinforced for her on a daily basis. She continues to experience increased energy until late at night, with no low spots during her day no matter how hectic. Patricia also continues to be completely free from the debilitating effects of colitis.

We were interested to read in the *"False Fat Diet"* by Dr. Elson M. Haas that wheat is one of seven foods to which many people react. The other foods that people often react adversely to are dairy products, corn, sugar, eggs, soy and peanuts. It is quite possible to be sensitive to foods without being truly allergic to them. So, although you may not go into shock when you eat these foods, you may experience symptoms like indigestion, bowel problems, headaches, sore throat, swollen glands and others. Dr. Haas feels eating foods we are sensitive to stresses our immune system. This weakens our response to stimuli such as pollens and other environmental influences. If you feel that you may have some food sensitivities impacting your health, this book is a good source of information. Dr. Haas outlines an elimination diet to help you determine whether you react to foods. We were interested to read that Dr. Haas feels 'cravings' for a particular food can be an indication of a sensitivity to this food.

We have had readers write to us about using a low carb approach to eating, not for weight loss, but for other health reasons. Research has shown that a low carbohydrate approach to food will have a positive effect on the health of diabetics, and may prevent the onset of adult diabetes. We have heard from readers who do not have the energy that they used to have, or feel they should have, wondering if adopting a low carb lifestyle will provide renewed energy. There have been readers who, like Patricia, suffer from digestive concerns and wonder whether a low carb approach would be of benefit to them. There have been readers who have suffered headaches and mood swings, asking whether diet and controlling carbohydrates would help alleviate these symptoms. In virtually every case, reducing the level of carbohydrate intake has had dramatic, positive results. Not only will you have more energy during the day once you have made the transition to a low carb lifestyle, but it is likely that you will sleep better and wake up in the morning feeling refreshed and ready for your day. You will notice a renewed vigor and enthusiasm for life.

Reducing carbohydrates when weight loss is not an issue is somewhat easier because the carbohydrate intake does not need to be as low as it does for weight loss. This approach allows greater flexibility and options such as eating more fruit initially. It allows consumption of some whole grain products if wheat is not a concern for the individual. We present more details about these options in Chapter 7, Menu Planning.

"Patricia Haakonson's cookbook, Everyday Low Carb Cooking*,
has helped me improve my overall health. I first purchased the
book for a friend who needed to lose weight. I was interested in
the book because I have known Patricia for many years, and was
amazed to see how wonderful she looked during a recent visit to
Victoria. Before I actually gave my friend the book, I began to
read it myself, just out of curiosity. I have never had a weight
problem, however I wondered what type of 'diet tricks' this book
boasted. To my delight, I learned that this book was not about
'diet tricks'. It was common sense eating, simple recipes that
taste great, with ingredients that most of us have in our kitchens.
Not only were the recipes appealing, but Patricia's discovery that
by reducing her carbs, she eliminated the symptoms of Colitis led*

me to believe that perhaps I could be helped. I have suffered all my life from Irritable Bowel Syndrome (IBS) and have never had much success in treating it. Because I didn't want to lose weight, with Patricia's counsel, I added fruit and extra portions to my meals, but I stayed away from the refined carbs. Since following this approach to food I have not suffered from my IBS, except of course, when I cheat! Delighted with the results, I purchased another book for my friend Barb. She and her husband both followed Patricia's advice, and have both lost weight without feeling deprived! They are now, like me, true believers in this healthy eating lifestyle!"
Jacqueline McDonald, Toronto, Ontario, Canada

*Now available under the title, *Easy Low Carb Cooking*.

Food Guidelines

The following guidelines are important when following a low carb approach to food, whether for weight loss or maintenance. Please read the guidelines carefully and try to adhere to the principles presented.

Do *not* skip breakfast. It is an important start to your day. Caffeine stimulates insulin production in the body, so you may wish to switch to decaffeinated coffee in the morning. Patricia has one or two cups of regular coffee first thing in the morning, and then switches to decaff for the balance of the day. If you want to lighten your coffee, add a small amount of light cream (not the flavored creams). If you prefer some sweetener, we recommend the use of Splenda.

All fruits and vegetables contain carbohydrates. We have provided separate lists of the high and low carbohydrate fruits and vegetables in the next section. Do not eat any potatoes, rice, pasta or bread while on the weight loss plan. We do not recommend that you eat any popcorn, candy or sweet desserts other than sugar free jello during the weight loss period.

Drink at least 8 full glasses of water every day. As with all weight loss plans, this is important to keep your body hydrated, and to facilitate the flushing of waste products. If you do not like the taste of tap water, try filtered water, bottled water or soda water. Drink herb tea in any quantity or flavor. These teas also help to make you feel more full.

Diet drinks with artificial sweeteners sometimes act as a trigger for hunger. You will have to decide if your body reacts to them. Most diet drinks contain aspartame and there are individuals who react adversely to aspartame, experiencing headaches or other symptoms when they consume diet drinks. Fresca, which is the soft drink we prefer, also contains aspartame. We find it a refreshing alternative to soda water, and it has 0 calories and 0 carbs. We do not react to aspartame and probably average only 1 or 2 diet drinks in a week.

You may use garnishes including garlic, herbs, mustard, real mayonnaise, olives, salt & pepper, or vinegar. Do *not* use ketchup, jams, mint jelly or apple sauce, all of which contain sugar and therefore are very high in carbs.

You need to exercise caution in the preparation of salads. A green salad of lettuce, celery and cucumber will have very few carbohydrates until you add salad dressing. If you add too many extra vegetables, such as sweet green peppers or tomatoes, you may dramatically increase the carbohydrate content of the meal. Be sure to check the carbohydrate counter for the carb content of vegetables, until you are more familiar with this approach to meal preparation. Be sure to check the carb content of your dressing.

Coleslaw has very few carbs. Patricia developed 4 different coleslaw recipes for her cookbook and we use them as a staple for lunch, rather than salads. An additional benefit with coleslaw is it will keep in the fridge for 2 or 3 days, even after it has been dressed. This means that low carb foods are in the fridge and readily available all the time.

We are often asked for a list of the high carb foods that should be avoided on a low carb diet. Many people do not understand what constitutes low or high carb foods. People often ask what do you eat, if you eliminate carbohydrates? As we have previously stated, it is virtually impossible to eliminate carbohydrates from your diet, and we do not recommend that you try. Almost all foods, with the exception of meat, poultry and fish, have carbohydrates. It is a matter of choosing foods with lower carb content and where possible, a low glycemic index. Don't worry about getting too technical. Review the following two lists and try to manage your food intake around the basic guidelines presented. The foods in the first list should be avoided during any weight loss period. Some of them may be carefully reintroduced in small quantities during the maintenance period. You can refer to the Easy Carbohydrate Counter in Chapter 12 to determine the carb content of any food.

High Carb Foods

Baked goods, especially sweets (pies, cakes, cookies, doughnuts)
Breads, especially white breads, including bagels, muffins, scones
Candy
Cereal, either hot or cold
Corn, carrots, beets, peas, beans, & lentils (these vegetables are naturally high in sugar and therefore high in carbs)
Fruit juices of any kind, other than lime or lemon
Most fruits, particularly bananas, apples, & oranges (at least initially)
Pasta
Potatoes, sweet potatoes
Rice, especially white rice
Sugar

Low Carb Foods

This list represents the foods that are naturally lower in carbs. These can be eaten during the weight loss period.

Cheese, cottage cheese (dry curd, creamed or 4% fat), yogurt (whole)
Chicken, turkey
Eggs and egg substitutes
Fish, shellfish
Lettuce, celery, cucumber, all sprouts, garlic, swiss chard, okra, spinach, mushrooms, cabbage, cauliflower, asparagus, avocado, broccoli, green beans, yellow beans, zucchini, eggplant, summer squash, spaghetti squash

Lemons, limes and their juices
Meat, including bacon
Nuts and seeds (in moderation)
Strawberries, raspberries, blackberries, kiwi fruit, grapefruit, or peaches (all in small quantities)
Tofu

Drinks

Drink at least 8 glasses of water a day to help flush your system and keep your kidneys working well. Drinking lots of water will also help to keep your stomach feeling fuller and will ensure that you don't dehydrate. Patricia likes to drink sparkling water, often with a wedge of lime for a bit of extra flavor. Harv prefers just ice cold water. Whatever your preference, be sure to get plenty of water.

If you drink alcohol it must always be in moderation. We are both non-drinkers, as a matter of choice. Some alcohol consumption during the weight loss phase is possible if quantities are controlled. Please refer to the carb counter at the back of this book to look up references. A glass of wine is the best choice from a carbohydrate perspective. As with other weight loss plans, if you consume mixed drinks, it is the mix that will provide the high carbohydrates and counteract all your hard work.

It is generally recommended that you refrain from caffeinated drinks while on the weight loss portion of a low carbohydrate plan. Caffeine will stimulate the pancreas to produce insulin, which is counterproductive and may stimulate hunger. Patricia does have a cup or two of regular coffee in the morning and then switches to decaff for the rest of the day. We both drink herb teas that are naturally decaffeinated. Recent research suggests that regular teas contribute to the formation of kidney stones, so you may want to curb your consumption of regular teas, if you have any history of kidney stones.

Whether you choose to drink any soft drinks is entirely up to you. What is important is that you make an informed decision. A single can of Coke has approximately 42 grams of carbohydrate in it – more than is recommended for your entire daily intake during weight loss. Diet drinks do not have any carbohydrates, but most of them still contain aspartame as the sweetening agent. Some diet soft drink manufacturers in Canada have switched to Splenda as the sweetening agent but you have to check the label to be sure. As discussed in the following section, some people react adversely to aspartame, experiencing a variety of symptoms including headaches, indigestion, sleep disturbances, and difficulty concentrating. Crystal Light is a powdered drink available in a variety of flavors that many people enjoy in lieu of fruit juices. Crystal Light also contains aspartame. You can make an informed decision regarding whether you want to drink anything that contains a sugar substitute.

Sugar Substitutes

There are a number of sugar substitutes on the market. The one we use and recommend is sucralose, marketed under the name of Splenda. It is our opinion that none of the other options offer any advantage over Splenda and most have definite disadvantages. We review all of the major options below.

Sucralose (Splenda)

Splenda is made from sugar and is actually sucralose, a sugar derivative. The chemical process that converts sugar to sucralose changes the sugar molecule so it cannot be digested by the body thus it does not stimulate the release of insulin. Splenda does not change either its consistency or its flavor when heated, which makes it suitable for baking and cooking. Splenda is the sugar substitute that has been recommended by Health Magazine. There is no aspartame in Splenda.

Splenda is available in three or four forms, depending on your location. The liquid form is not currently available in North America, although there is some lobbying going on to convince the company to make it available. The other forms that are readily available are 1) small individual packets, 2) loose granular form (in a box), and 3) individual tablets for hot drinks. Patricia uses the packets for convenience when cooking. The Splenda in the packets is in concentrated form, and is equivalent to two teaspoons of sugar. Granulated Splenda is not concentrated, and may be used in quantities equal to sugar when substituting in a favorite recipe. Harv uses the granular form when sprinkling it on his oatmeal and the tablet form in his tea.

Aspartame (Equal)

Until Splenda came along, aspartame was by far the most widely used artificial sweetener. It had replaced saccharin largely because it did not stimulate the release of insulin. A minor drawback is that it does not remain stable when heated so it cannot be used in cooking. A more serious problem is the number of potential side effects including headaches, indigestion, sleep disturbances, dizziness, and difficulty concentrating.

By far the greatest concern about aspartame is the growing scientific evidence of risk to the brain and nervous system. There has not yet been sufficient proof to be certain of this hazard but there is enough evidence to suggest it is wise to avoid the use of aspartame as much as possible. Be aware that it is still widely used as an artificial sweetener, especially in soft drinks.

As an aside, the mechanism of action that makes aspartame a risk to the brain and nervous system is the same mechanism that causes concern with monosodium glutamate (MSG).

Saccharin (Sweet'N Low)

This is the oldest of the artificial sweeteners (discovered in 1879) and though it was mostly replaced by aspartame, it probably is still a better option. It has few side effects and remains stable when heated so can be used in cooking. A major disadvantage is that it stimulates the pancreas to release insulin. Laboratory studies using high doses in rats did produce bladder cancer but this has never happened in humans. In our opinion there is minimal health risk if you occasionally need to use Sweet'N Low as your sweetener.

Cyclamate (Sugar Twin, Sucaryl)

Cyclamate remains stable in heat so is useful for cooking. This product is available in Canada but remains banned in the United States because of concerns about bladder cancer in rats. This has never been shown in humans after 30 years of study. We do not think there is any serious risk to health with the occasional use of this sweetener.

Stevia

This is a natural sweetener sold primarily in health food stores. It remains stable in liquids and heat so can be used to sweeten drinks or for cooking and baking. It does have a slight licorice flavor that complicates its use. It is also very sweet which can complicate determining the proper amount to use in a recipe. It can stimulate the release of insulin so should be used sparingly.

Sugar Alcohols (sorbitol, maltitol, xylitol)

These products are not absorbed from the intestine so they do not stimulate the release of insulin. They tend to get used in 'diabetic' candies and gums. A definite caution is that their action in the large intestine can cause diarrhea. Many sugar free chocolate products contain sugar alcohols.

Food Triggers

Many of us have 'food triggers'. A food trigger can be an event, an activity, an emotion, or a food or food type. A food trigger makes us want to eat (or to binge) when we are not hungry. There has been a lot of talk in recent years about eating disorders and unhealthy attitudes towards food. We all, from time to time, use food for enjoyment or comfort, and not simply to nourish our bodies. We want you to enjoy your food. We want you to be aware that some situations may be more difficult for you to maintain your resolve. Can you identify your food triggers? Patricia knows that watching television is a food trigger for her, so she is careful to limit any snacks during TV time. She also has discovered that she has problems limiting her consumption of cashews, so we no longer keep them in the house. Pay attention to your eating. Take precautions against any food or situation that might lead you to overindulge.

Weight Loss Plateau

It is common to experience a period during which we 'stall' in our weight loss. We are not 100% sure of the mechanism that causes the stall, but there are some things that can be done to counteract this 'leveling out'. It is important to try to determine what has caused the stall. Sometimes it might be that our body is taking a few days (or weeks) to adjust to our new lifestyle. It might be that we have started eating foods that we should avoid, or that we have become a little complacent in our low carb plan. It might also be that quantities have been slowly increasing, especially with our snack foods. Sometimes it might be a particular food that is the culprit. The foods that might be responsible will vary with each individual, based on our metabolisms and our preferences.

There are many foods that can cause a stall in weight loss, and the determination of which ones affect you might require some trial and error on your part. Maybe you know which foods these are. One of the likely suspects are the commercial low carb bars, if you have decided to include them as a regular part of your plan. We suggest you cut these out first, if you are eating them as a normal part of your weight loss plan, and experience a stall.

Other foods that can cause stalls include anything with a high salt content, including any salted nuts, salted seeds, and pork rinds. Monitor your intake carefully and if you stall, review the foods that you have been consuming, particularly the snack foods. If you want to continue to eat nuts you may chose to try the roasted, but unsalted variety, or try natural, raw nuts & seeds. Some individuals report that foods with artificial sweeteners can cause stalls or trigger cravings for additional sweets. You will have to be the judge of whether these foods are inappropriate for you.

Lack of exercise, or a dramatic shift in your daily activity level, can also contribute to a stall in weight loss. Your food diary, where you also keep track of your activity levels, will help you determine if this has contributed to your stall. If you are not eating enough to satisfy your hunger at meals, you may be eating more snacks than you intend, and this might contribute to your stall. A careful review of your food diary will highlight this.

Once you have determined what might be the cause of your stall, you need to change something in your approach. If you think that you can identify the culprit (for example too many low carb bars), then the change is obvious. If it is not immediately obvious what has caused the stall, you need to engage in a process of trial and error to see if you can identify the culprit. Are you getting enough exercise? If not, try adding a walk at noon everyday; a 20 minute walk on a daily basis will make a difference. Are you snacking in the evening after dinner? Try some sugar free jello as a snack, or some sugar free gum to avoid snacks before bed.

What you want to do is *change* some aspect of your plan to 'kick start' the weight loss again. Sometimes it might mean reducing your daily carb intake to something just a bit lower, to get that metabolism back into high gear. Or maybe you need to add some additional vegetables (the low carb type) and salads to help fill your tummy and add bulk to your meals. And, sometimes you just need to be patient. We have known individuals to stall for as many as 6 or 8 weeks for no apparent reason, and then suddenly start losing again. If you are patient, it will happen. And, even if you are in a stall, if you are faithful to the low carb approach, you will be maintaining your weight and not gaining, which is a positive result. Don't give up! A stall is a temporary thing. Do not lose faith in your new low carb lifestyle. Keep your consumption of carbs to the level that you have determined works best, and you will be rewarded.

Physical Activity

Anyone starting a low carb lifestyle should visit their family physician to ensure there is no risk to their health if they adopt this new food plan. We also recommend that everyone, whether dieting or not, should have a daily vitamin and mineral supplement and engage in regular physical activity.

The health benefits from regular physical activity are substantial. Dr. Willett states (p.49): "Other than not smoking, exercise is the single best thing you can do to get healthy or stay healthy and keep chronic diseases at bay." Physical activity can:

- Be fun
- Make your body look better
- Help you to lose weight by burning calories
- Increase your metabolic rate
- Increase your energy
- Add muscle, which burns more calories

- Reduce the output of insulin
- Improve your chances of living longer and living healthier
- Help protect you from developing heart disease
- Help protect you from developing high blood pressure and high cholesterol
- Help protect you from developing some cancers, including colon and breast
- Help prevent adult onset diabetes
- Help prevent arthritis
- Relieve the pain and stiffness in people with arthritis
- Help prevent osteoporosis
- Reduce the risk of falling in older adults
- Relieve symptoms of depression and anxiety
- Improve mood

The important role of regular physical activity during weight loss deserves special discussion. The most obvious benefit is the calories 'burned up' while being physically active, calories that would otherwise end up as stored fat. Less obvious is the benefit from the growth in muscle size. Even while you sleep your muscles continue to use energy (calories). The more muscle mass you have, the more calories get burned while you sleep. Regular physical activity results in growth in the strength and size (mass) of your muscles. The more you exercise, the more muscle mass you have to work for you while you sleep.

The questions always arise concerning what kind of exercise is best, and how much exercise is optimal? The first really important message is there is no need to think that you have to join a gym, or start lifting weights, or attend step classes, to participate in effective physical activity. Brisk walking is one of the best exercises and requires only a good pair of walking shoes and a commitment to be effective. Dr. Willett reported (p.51) that in the Nurses' Health Study, women who walked an average of three hours per week at a brisk pace were 35% less likely to have a heart attack over an eight year period than women who walked infrequently. Barry Sears, author of *"The Zone"* explains "What is the best exercise to achieve this? (fat burning) It's called walking." (p.58) A 30-minute daily walk will go a long way to helping you take off, and keep off, those extra pounds.

Patricia is a 52 year old, post-menopausal woman with osteoarthritis. She is unable to run, due to the joint pain that she experiences when she tries. She can, however, walk briskly for 30 to 45 minutes without any discomfort. She does so religiously, with her walkman attached to her belt and her favorite music playing to help her maintain a brisk pace. Harv prefers to run. At the age of 60, he decided to train for his first ever marathon – a 26.2 mile test of endurance and will. He has now run two marathons and continues to run a 6 mile course, four times a week. It is interesting to note that Harv trained for six months to run the Boston Marathon (which he finished in just 3:35:37) while following a modified low carbohydrate diet and eating foods exclusively out of Patricia's cookbook, *Easy Low Carb Cooking*.

CHAPTER 5

Getting Started

"The ultimate diet would be one that controls hunger, is pleasing and satisfying, meets the body's needs for energy and nutrients, and minimizes the risk of chronic disease. That's a tall order."

Walter C. Willett, M.D.

We recommend you finish this book before starting your journey into the world of low carb lifestyles. If you do, you will have a better understanding of all aspects of the decision you are making, and how to prepare yourself and your family to ensure success. The decision to try a low carb approach to eating had a dramatic impact on our lives, and we are certain that it will have a similar impact on yours. In our experience a simple approach to starting your low carb lifestyle and tracking your success works best.

Food Diary

It is extremely important to record your food intake, and the grams of carbohydrate, on a daily basis. This written record is known as a food diary and it is an essential tool for you in determining the level of carbohydrate intake that best suits your needs and your lifestyle. This record will demonstrate to you exactly how many carbohydrates you can tolerate and still lose weight or maintain your desired weight. The associated general health benefits will accrue in either instance.

Keeping track of your food and maintaining a written account is not as difficult as it sounds. We have provided a simple format for you to use in the initial weeks of your low carb plan. Recording your food will bring a measure of discipline to the low carb approach that is particularly helpful in the early stages. We record the food we eat to create an accurate record so we can determine how many carbs we consume on average in a week. This information allows us to determine what our individual tolerances are with respect to grams of carbohydrate and weight loss or weight maintenance. Although there are general guidelines concerning how many carbs should be consumed in a day on a weight loss plan, our experience has shown that the guidelines are just that. They are not hard and fast rules that must be followed in order to achieve the desired results. Individual differences will occur regarding tolerance levels. You will discover that the lower your carbohydrate consumption, the quicker the weight loss. It is very simple.

To track your daily carbohydrate consumption, use a format similar to the one presented in Chapter 11 of this book. We have provided a sufficient number of pages for you to record the first two weeks of low carb eating. You will find a 'downloadable' version of the food diary on our website at www.lowcarbliving.ca The form that your food diary takes is not nearly as important as the information it contains. We are trying to make things easy for you by providing examples that work for us. Any format you chose to make for yourself will work, as long as the essential information is there.

In our experience, the food diary will be most useful if it contains the following elements.

The **Daily** information should include:
♦ Date
♦ Space to record all the food eaten, separated into meals and snacks
♦ Space to record the grams of carbohydrate for each food, plus total
♦ Space to record any exercise or activity
♦ Space for notes or remarks

The **Weekly Summary** should include:
- Daily carbs and exercise, plus weekly average
- Weekly weigh-in information
- Comments

We don't carry a food diary with us everywhere we go. This seems tedious and intrusive. We want this plan to be simple and easy, as well as effective. We usually spend a couple of minutes in the evening, either while dinner is cooking or while we enjoy tea after dinner to review what we have eaten during the day. It gets easy to remember, once you are in the habit. To accurately record the grams of carbohydrate, you will probably find that you need to look up values in our Easy Carbohydrate Counter until you become more familiar with them. It took us a while to learn the carbohydrate count of the foods we eat on a regular basis. Once you learn the carb content of the foods you consume regularly, you will be able to keep your daily food diary without looking up the values. We have provided a basic carbohydrate counter in Chapter 12 to get you started. We have not tried to be exhaustive in our carb counter, but to provide you with the means to look up most common daily foods.

As with other weight loss and weight management programs, the body will sometimes adapt or adjust to the new level of food intake. This can trigger what is often called a 'stall'. You may stop loosing weight and seem to be stalled at a weight that is more than your goal weight. The food diary is particularly useful in helping you determine what sort of strategy or change is necessary to 'kick-start' the weight loss again. Patricia had one week during her initial 3 month weight loss period when she put on 2 pounds. This was very uncharacteristic for her, and an examination of her daily diary enabled her to identify why this happened and how to avoid a subsequent weight gain. Harv is not quite as steady in his carbohydrate intake as Patricia, and we see a direct correlation between his occasional increases in consumption and fluctuations in his weight.

The discipline that keeping a food diary involves is particularly important at the beginning when you are making major changes in your habits and adjusting to a whole new way of thinking about foods. When you sit at the end of the day and record what foods you have eaten, and then look up and record the grams of carb you have consumed, you will quickly realize how your day has gone. Patricia totals our carb count at the end of every day. We then review whether it has been a 'low', 'normal' or 'high' day with respect to our carbohydrate intake. Everyone has the occasional high day. The beauty of keeping a diary on a daily basis is that you get immediate feedback, and can make the decision to have a 'low' day, the next day. This will help keep you on track and may avoid the disappointment of small gains during the weight loss period if you are attentive to your daily record keeping and what it tells you.

Weigh-Ins

Weigh yourself on a weekly basis, and record your weight. It will be most accurate if you pick one day of the week as your weigh-in day, such as Saturday or Sunday. Get up and weigh yourself first thing in the morning. We do not recommend that you weigh yourself on a daily basis. Weighing on a daily basis places too much emphasis on just the weight aspect of the low carb lifestyle. This may cause some individuals to experience anxiety each morning as they step on the scale. There will be daily fluctuations in weight that can be caused by many factors beyond actual weight loss. These fluctuations can be the result of fluid loss or retention or hormonal changes, rather than real weight gain or loss.

If you weigh yourself once weekly you will have an accurate record of your weight loss over time. We chart our weight on a weekly basis, with our daily average carbohydrate intake. This has allowed us to ascertain exactly how many carbs we can ingest on average without gaining weight. It can be extremely satisfying to look at the weight chart over time and see how successful you have been, if weight loss is your primary goal.

If weight maintenance is your primary goal, it is still important to weigh yourself and record the weight to ensure that you are not losing or gaining any significant amounts without knowing about it. Patricia occasionally loses an additional 2 to 3 pounds if she has a very active week and burns up more energy than usual. Without a regular schedule of weigh-ins, she would not have any method to alert her to this small loss. Her carbohydrate intake is so steady and instinctive, after two years of eating a maintenance level of low carb, that increased activity levels will cause additional weight loss. If this happens, Patricia simply increases her carbohydrate intake the following week (often with the addition of extra fruit servings) to regain those few pounds. Such a small loss, if it happens on an isolated basis, is not a major concern. However, if you have successive weeks of high activity levels and the associated losses, you might find yourself below your ideal weight.

We recently had a five day trip to the city of Vancouver. Patricia was busy walking around the downtown core to visit various bookstores, while Harv had a few days of meetings to attend. We stayed in a little hotel that offered a continental breakfast to its guests. Patricia decided not to indulge and she continued her habit of a low carb shake and coffee for breakfast each day. Harv enjoyed a muffin and orange juice every morning, and he ate sandwiches that were brought into the meetings every day for lunch. Patricia stopped each day for lunch to have a salad with chicken strips or a hamburger (without the bun). We went out to dinner every evening, and made similar choices about our foods. Harv was experimenting with his carb intake. After five days of this type of eating, Patricia lost an additional 2 pounds due to all the extra walking, and Harv put on 5 pounds due to the additional intake of carbs!

We have provided a simple tool to assist you in recording your weight during the initial stages of your low carb plan. This tool is located in Chapter 11, Your Personal Food Diary. Routine is an important strategy in establishing habits. This is why it is important that you get on the scale first thing in the morning on the same day each week. We have found that doing so on a weekend morning is easy to remember.

Identify Your Goals

As with most endeavors, it is easier to track your progress if you clearly identify your goals and record milestones. It may be as simple as 'I want to lose 20 pounds'. Perhaps you are still unsure about a low carb approach, and want to experiment for a two week period. You can then assess the impact of eating low carb. We are confident that if you do, you will want to continue with your low carb plan. The health benefits and initial weight loss will become obvious within a week or ten days, if you are faithful to the low carb approach to eating.

When Patricia first started eating low carb her goal was to lose weight. Within 10 days she had another goal, having decided that she would never go back to her previous way of eating. Patricia determined that she would adopt a low carbohydrate lifestyle. This decision was based on two dramatic changes in her health status; a significant increase in energy and the elimination of her symptoms of colitis. It may be that you have considerable weight to lose, or a wedding to attend where you want to look great. It may be that your doctor has cautioned you to lose weight for medical reasons, or you want to avoid adult onset diabetes. Perhaps you are seeking to improve your overall health.

Whatever your reasons you will find it easier to adhere to your plan if you have a *written* record of your goals. When you feel you might be heading towards a lack of resolve, go back to your goals and remind yourself why you decided to start a low carb plan. When friends or family are less supportive than you would like, support yourself by referring to your goals, and your success in working toward them. One day, you will look at these goals and realize that they have been achieved.

Create a Safe & Supportive Environment

There are many things that you can do to make your home or office a 'safe' low carb environment. The exact approach will vary depending on whether you live and eat alone, or are responsible for feeding a family. It is important to ensure that the foods you want to consume are readily available. It is equally important that the people you live with and care about are supportive of your efforts.

One of the first things to do is ensure the kitchen cupboards, and the fridge, contain low carb foods that are safe for you. Even snack foods need to be of the low carb variety, such as hard boiled eggs or pork rinds. You will find lists of appropriate low carb snacks in Chapter 7 on Menu Planning. Go through your kitchen cupboards and remove all the packaged baked goods, all the cake mixes, the potato chips, the corn chips and popcorn. Take away any crackers and dry cereals, cookies, pretzels and pasta as well. There are a couple of choices regarding how you dispose of these foods.

If you have a family to feed you may need to ensure they have access to the foods and snacks they want, without tempting you to 'just have one' of anything. If your family wants access to high carb foods, perhaps you can reorganize your kitchen cupboards so all the high carb food is kept in one cupboard. You can avoid being tempted, by not going into that cupboard. If you don't have a family to feed, you can choose to give this food to the food bank or to neighbors and friends. This ensures that it doesn't get wasted and doesn't get eaten by you! One reader from Patricia's cookbook wrote that she and her husband were thrilled with the results of eating low carb. The reader wondered what to do with all the high carb food in her freezer and then suggested she might have a party and let all her friends eat it for her! Good idea!

When Patricia first started the low carb diet, Harv was not sure he wanted to participate. How we dealt with this was to prepare high carb foods for Harv that Patricia didn't care for. In this way, Harv had his high carb foods when he wanted them, but Patricia was not tempted to eat them. Within a short period of time, Harv stopped wanting potatoes and other high carb foods. Partially this was because the rest of the meal was so delicious and plentiful he didn't feel the need for high carb extras. In addition, Patricia's results were so spectacular that Harv decided to try it out for himself. Now, our understanding of the impact of high carbohydrate foods on our health is enough motivation for us both.

It is easier to prepare and consume meals if you don't have to deal with potatoes and other high carb foods. But, it is possible to prepare these foods for your family, and refrain from eating them yourself. If you can do this for even a short period of time, you will be so amazed and pleased with the results that you will find it easier to continue to exercise good judgement and control over your carbohydrate intake. In Chapter 7 on Menu Planning, we provide a basic weekly grocery list for low carb living. This will help you to shop more successfully, especially when you are new to the art of low carb meal preparation.

Tell your family, and close friends if you are confident of their support, what you are doing and how important it is to have their support. There has been some criticism of low carb diets in the news over the past few years. While we are convinced that low carb eating will become more mainstream as the research results are made public, you may have to deal with friends or family who are skeptical or even negative about your new approach to eating. There are a number of approaches you can take in response to this type of concern. Perhaps the simplest would be to explain that while you appreciate their concern, you feel you have done the appropriate research and this approach is a healthy alternative for you. If it is a partner or spouse who seems somewhat less than supportive, you might hand them this book when you have finished reading it and ask them to read certain chapters. Or perhaps you will want to tell them that they don't need to understand it or even try it, but that you would like them to support you in your efforts. We are confident that if you are able to stick to a low carb weight loss plan for two weeks you and your family will notice the results.

There will be others who are not family or close friends who might not be interested in trying to understand this approach to food and its health benefits. You may decide that educating them is a time commitment you don't want to make. In this case you need to learn to disregard any negative comments. You might remind yourself that they are probably speaking out of ignorance and a lack of knowledge. You can reassure yourself that you have done the necessary homework to feel confident in your choices.

There will be friends and acquaintances who, for whatever reason, and perhaps unknowingly, will try to sabotage your efforts by dropping by with some warm cinnamon buns just at coffee break. Perhaps a friend will entreat you to 'just take one little bite' of something that you know is not good for you. You will have to learn to refuse with a joke or a smile. There is no use getting upset. You probably won't change these individuals. You can smile and feel self satisfied as they start to notice the changes in your appearance and your energy level, as you progress with your low carb plan.

Unfortunately people sometimes think that *our* behavior is a comment on *their* behavior. By this we mean that when we decide not to have a muffin at coffee break, others assume that we are suggesting that they shouldn't either and they may become defensive. One way to defuse this sort of situation is to simply state that you believe you have a 'sensitivity' to wheat and you feel you are healthier when you don't eat baked goods. The fact that you are losing weight is simply a nice bonus!

Once you have decided to follow a low carb approach to eating, and you explain the how and why to your family and close friends, you are ready to embark on a wonderful journey. Within a remarkably short period of time you will begin to see and feel results that will support your decision and help you be motivated to continue. Some days will be easier than others, as with any new endeavor. Just do the best you can to stick to your plan. If you feel you need some additional support there are a number of ideas that we can suggest, including our website, www.lowcarbliving.ca and other websites that provide a forum for discussion, and information about research and new products. We will explore some of these in detail in Chapter 10 on Low Carb Products and Resources.

Just Do It

Once you have decided to start a low carbohydrate approach to eating, there is no reason to hesitate. The low carb approach to food requires some changes in the way you think about food and diet, and you may need to get a load of 'low carb' groceries, but beyond that, there is little else you need in the way of additional equipment or preparation. We started on the weekend so our Day One in the food diary is always a Sunday. You can start any day of the week and any date on the calendar.

We have met people who are interested in the low carb approach to eating for weight loss, but not quite committed to it. The weight loss will only be effective in the long term, if you take a serious approach to the carb content of your foods. It is self-defeating behavior to announce that you have decided to eat a low carb diet, but can't or won't give up bread or potatoes. This will not be effective and will be demotivating for you when you do your weekly weigh-in. We once traveled with friends who were 'on a low carb diet'. These friends were not committed to this approach, and at every meal they would eat a roll or potato, which they justified with the comment, "I'll just have this little treat today and then no more tomorrow." Tomorrow never comes, and these friends lost faith in the low carb approach to weight loss. The simple fact is they never were on a low carb program. They didn't think it necessary to keep a food diary so they perhaps didn't realize how the carbs were creeping up on them.

Patricia loved breads and potatoes when she started her weight loss program and was worried about being able to stick to the low carb approach. She used a bit of reverse psychology with herself and it seemed to work well. Patricia got up each morning for the first two weeks and promised herself that if she stuck to the low carb program today, she would allow herself the 'reward' of a bagel tomorrow. As with our friends in the previous paragraph, tomorrow never came for Patricia. She never did 'reward' herself with any high carb foods and so was extremely successful with her weight loss. One of the most interesting things that she noted was, she soon stopped thinking of those high carb foods and didn't feel that she was missing anything. A low carb program that is well thought out with variety and flavor is absolutely as satisfying as eating high carb. You may find that you begin to enjoy the taste of vegetables more and lose your taste for potatoes and bread. You may notice food 'cravings' you used to have will disappear.

Once you decide to start your low carb plan, 'just do it'. You will want to weigh yourself at the start so you can accurately reflect your progress, and you might need to get a load of low carb groceries. You don't need to announce it to the world. This can be stressful to some people, if you think that friends and acquaintances are watching to see what progress you make. We do recommend that you discuss your decision with your family so they can best support your efforts, as previously discussed.

The Critical First Steps

+ Make your commitment.
+ Determine your goal and write it down.
+ Keep a food diary of your old carbohydrate habits for a week before you start.
+ Get a load of low carb groceries.
+ Weigh yourself (then weigh-in at the same time every week).
+ Just DO IT!

CHAPTER 6

Strategies For Success

"You can eat the natural healthy animal and vegetable foods that people ate and grew robust on in centuries past."
Robert C. Atkins, M.D.

This chapter provides ideas to help you achieve your goals more easily. These methods and ideas were developed using a system of trial and error. When we initially decided to try a low carb approach to eating, it was very foreign to us. The shift from low fat meals and food preparation was not easy or instinctive. Some of these strategies were outlined in the first edition of Patricia's cookbook, *Easy Low Carb Cooking* (previously titled *Everyday Low Carb Cooking*). Patricia has received considerable feedback regarding how helpful the strategies are in making the adjustment to a low carb lifestyle.

"The most convincing part of Patricia's cookbook, Everyday Low Carb Cooking,* *was the introduction. Patricia wrote about everyday things that we need to consider when eating a low carb/ no sugar diet. As an example, she gave helpful (realistic) hints on what to eat/drink when visiting with friends.*
The recipes are all fabulous but my favorite is the BBQ Spare Ribs. My family loves them and my friends all want the recipe. They can't believe that it comes from a low carb cookbook. I guess people still believe that if you are on a special diet, you have to give up all the flavors you love and eat boring, dull, unappetizing food. Patricia's cookbook dispels all of those myths and even gives the reader interesting ideas to try new things.

Who would ever think of substituting cauliflower for mashed potatoes?

To date, I've lost 20 pounds. I am 5' 7" and started at a weight of 163 lbs. Yup, unbelievable, but true! I was carrying most of those pounds on my back, hips and thighs. Of course, now that I've lost all that weight, and maintained it for the last 4 months, I feel fabulous! I look fabulous too! Even my co-workers are noticing and are commenting on how good I look (the guys too)!

Of course, everyone wants to know 'What I did.' I don't hesitate to promote Patricia's cookbook and your way of eating. I also point out that the "Introduction" is the BEST part of the book. It helped convince me that 'I can really do this'."

Sheila Bernardi, Calgary, Alberta, Canada

*Now available as *Easy Low Carb Cooking*.

Meal Planning

Once you have decided that you are going to embark on a low carb plan (whether for weight loss, weight maintenance or general health concerns), created a safe environment, and bought a load of low carb groceries, you are ready to begin. You will find that meal planning is especially necessary if the low carb approach is going to work for you. Whether you work outside the home or stay at home to work, or are retired, you need to plan your food and your meals to ensure that you don't get caught with only high carb options when you are hungry. You can no longer afford to arrive home feeling famished, if you don't have some low carb options available in the fridge. A peanut butter sandwich just doesn't work anymore!

Second only to learning the carbohydrate content of everyday foods, meal planning is the strategy that will be most helpful to you in your program. Planning is necessary both from the perspective of the foods that are available in the fridge, and the menu that is being prepared. Menus and foods will vary depending on whether you are on a weight loss program or maintenance, but the principles remain the same. A daily plan outlining foods for breakfast, lunch, dinner and a couple of snacks will facilitate your ability to maintain your low carb plan. Meal planning can be done on a daily basis, or weekly, if you are very organized. Meal planning doesn't need to be written down or elaborate, as long as you know what you plan to eat for each meal. If done correctly, meal planning will help minimize the work involved in preparation, and maximize the benefits. Proper meal planning may also help contain the cost of food as there will be less waste and better use of left over foods.

It is easier to get up and get going in the morning if you have a plan for breakfast. We do not recommend that you start your day without nourishment. If you need to get up and make breakfast for other family members, or get off to a job, it is particularly important that you plan what you will eat so it can be accomplished without much effort. Whether you choose the option of bacon and eggs or a protein shake, having a plan will make it easier and less stressful for you in the morning, as you get ready for the rest of your day.

One of the simplest strategies we employ is to cook more protein than we will eat for our evening meal. This simple technique ensures that we always have protein available for lunches. Whether you eat lunch at home, at work, or at play (on the golf course!), having some cooked protein is the best start to making a quick and easy lunch. Once you have a small protein portion it is easy to add some salad or coleslaw, make a quick chicken salad or add a little cheese or nuts to round out your meal. How you proceed depends entirely on your preferences. Patricia has a number of specific suggestions in the menu planning section about how to make simple and quick lunches, snacks and even dinners.

If you are normally at home for lunch, and don't mind cooking, planning for lunch the day before is not quite as important. Although we are often at home, Patricia doesn't like to have to cook for lunch, so we generally pull out the left over protein from the evening before, and either re-heat it or eat it cold with whatever salads and vegetables are available and appropriate. An exception to this general rule of thumb might be during cold weather when we want hot soup for lunch.

We still make the evening meal our main meal of the day, although it is probably smaller than it used to be. We also eat relatively early in the evening to allow our food to digest before we retire. We have learned that lean muscle continues to burn small amounts of energy even during sleep. As your body becomes slimmer and you increase the amount of lean muscle tissue and decrease the adipose or fat tissue, you will become a more efficient energy burner, even in your sleep. Our evening meal typically contains a small salad or soup, a protein portion (fish, poultry or lean meat) and two vegetables. We often have some fruit or other low carb dessert to finish the meal, with either decaff coffee or herb tea. We always feel comfortably full and satisfied, but never stuffed! Make your meals interesting and tasty using recipes from Patricia's *Easy Low Carb Cooking.*

"In a world overwhelmed with complicated 'dieting solutions', from one extreme to another, these recipes are simple to prepare, the portions are very appropriate and the dishes are sprinkled with lightheartedness and delicate flavors. I particularly enjoyed the grilled halibut, which epitomizes Ms. Haakonson's style."
Dr. Walter G. Hartzell, Vancouver, British Columbia, Canada

It is important to plan for the snacks you will eat during your day. There are many weight loss diets that admonish you to eat only the meals that are prescribed, and not to snack in between meals. How many of us can do this and stick to it for very long? A more reasonable approach is to build the snacks into the meal plan. Patricia absolutely needs to have 3 snacks a day to avoid feeling constant hunger. So, that is what she does, planning her snacks as part of her overall food plan. Snacks may be necessary for a variety of reasons. If you expend a large amount of energy in a sport, gardening, or some other activity, you may need a small energy boost to get you to the next meal. If you have a longer than normal time period between meals, you may need a small snack to tide you over until the next meal. Sometimes snacks are a social necessity. If you work in an environment where your co-workers all go to coffee break together and have something to eat or drink, you will want to join them without sabotaging your weight loss. All of this can be accomplished with some planning. We will provide you with a long list of low carb snacks from which to choose. Remember to include your snacks in your daily food diary so you are being as accurate as possible with your carb count.

Eat Frequently & Eat Small

Most nutritionists will advise that it is better to eat a number of small meals throughout the day, rather than eat one large meal at the end of the day. Dr. Willett from Harvard makes this recommendation in his book. This is also part of our strategy as outlined in the foregoing paragraphs. We both eat between 4 and 6 times a day. This tends to include three satisfying meals and two or three snacks each day. We do not allow ourselves to get to the stage of feeling so hungry that we could 'eat a horse'. We have come to realize that we are choosing to eat smaller portions at all our meals, because we are less hungry due to the snacks we eat between meals. This is now part of our daily strategy to ensure that we have the energy we need all day long, without any of the highs and lows associated with eating high carb foods.

Our meals are not so small that it is apparent to the casual observer. If you were eating with us, you would not think that we were obviously 'dieting' because of the quantities that we eat. We have both remarked that our portions are somewhat smaller than they were before we started the low carb plan. Part of this is due to the fact that we used to consume bread with every meal and we no longer do. Nor have we felt the need to find a substitute for the bread. We have simply eliminated one food item from the meal. We eat lots of fresh vegetables and salads. This is a food type that has dramatically increased in our daily diet. It is also a food type that provides essential vitamins and minerals as well as fostering a slow release of sugar into the blood. We eat a variety of fresh fruits, and increased our consumption of fruits when we moved to maintenance. We do not go hungry. We *never* get up from the table feeling hungry.

The type of foods we choose for snacks has dramatically changed since beginning our low carb lifestyles. It is important to choose a snack food that will allow you to maintain an even blood sugar level, and therefore continue to feel alert and energetic. Eating low carb snack foods will help avoid the roller coaster ride of dramatic peaks in blood sugar after a high carb snack followed by dramatic drops in blood sugar when the pancreas kicks in to produce insulin.

Eating low carb snacks will provide you with a sense of satisfaction in terms of the hunger, but will also allow you to function without any of the negative results of a high carb snack. Chocolate bars, bagels or a bag of potato chips are no longer part of our diet. Our snacks typically include hard-boiled eggs, cheese, celery sticks, nuts and seeds and sometimes a low carb protein bar (more on these products later). There are many low carb options for snack foods. We have compiled a fairly extensive list in Chapter 7 on Menu Planning.

In complete harmony with most nutritionists, we recommend that you eat more frequently, and reduce the size of your portions at each setting. This will contribute to having a higher level of energy all day long and reduce any hunger or feelings of deprivation. It is important that you eat until you are satisfied. If at the end of the meal you are still feeling hungry, additional salad or more vegetables will help fill you up. When we first started to eat low carb we made the decision to serve two cooked vegetables with every meal, as well as a salad. This provides variety and flavor, as well as visual interest when the plate is in front of you. At the beginning, our vegetable servings were quite large, and they have gradually reduced in size as we became used to eating this way.

Eating Out

When we eat at home, it is easy to control our food intake. It is somewhat more difficult, but not impossible when eating out, either at the home of friends or in restaurants. Each situation requires a slightly different approach. We find that eating out at the home of friends can be more difficult than eating in a restaurant. In a restaurant there are many selections to choose from. In addition, the owner wants to look after your special needs to ensure you will return in the future. We begin with the invitation to eat at a friend's home.

We have two separate strategies we utilize when we go to the home of friends. One is to ask in a friendly way whether they feel up to the challenge of feeding us with our special requirements. Patricia has some severe food allergies, so it is quite appropriate to start with the elimination of these foods from the menu. We now include wheat in the list of allergies (although Patricia has a 'sensitivity' to wheat rather than a true allergy). This eliminates pasta as a main course, as well as bread and many high carb desserts. You might want to try this strategy yourself.

Our other strategy, while we are guests in someone else's home, is to eat very small portions of the foods that we normally don't eat at home. A perfect example would be white rice, which we never serve at home anymore. If a dinner plate is served at the home of friends that has white rice on it, we will have a small amount to avoid any insult or embarrassment. It is not going to harm your food plan or make a dramatic change in the results you seek, to occasionally eat something outside your normal choices. We sometimes eat a dessert made with sugar without any dramatic impact on our weight. We do this with the knowledge that our food intake for the next few days must reflect this indulgence. By this we mean that we are particularly careful with our food for a few days after a high carb dessert. An occasional indulgence will not do any harm, as long as it is only occasional and doesn't become habit.

Eating out in restaurants is very easy. We have gotten into the habit, especially if we are dining alone, of refusing the bread basket when it is brought to the table. There is no temptation to have a dinner roll, if there is no bread basket on the table. We always decline any potato or rice, and ask if we might have a few extra vegetables on the plate instead. We have never had our request refused, and we have occasionally had wonderful vegetable dishes substituted for potato. This can be done in a fast food restaurant as easily as in a fine dining establishment. They are only too pleased to look after their customer, in the hope of a return visit and good customer relations.

There are many low carb diets that admonish you to stay completely away from any food that has been breaded or battered and then fried. Patricia recalls reading in her research that eating any food that had wheat might trigger all the old 'cravings' that many people suffer while eating high carb foods. It has not been our experience that eating foods on occasion that have been breaded or battered and then deep fried trigger any kind of cravings or have any impact overall on the low carb plan. There are two examples in particular that Patricia likes to use. She loves to order fish and chips, without the chips! Our server often takes a second to understand that Patricia is asking for the deep fried fish and no potato. Patricia asks for some additional coleslaw or salad to make up for the potato, and has never been refused. She also likes to eat chicken tenders and orders them with a salad as a lunch meal if we are eating out. There have been no negative consequences to these choices in restaurants. We do not indulge in this type of food very often due to our concern about consuming the hydrogenated fats that are used in deep frying. Allow yourself to experiment with food that has been breaded and deep fried. We further recommend that you experiment slowly in this regard until you have had a little experience with your new eating habits and can make informed decisions about the impact of this type of food on your goals.

Traveling

Maintaining your low carb meal plan while traveling is more difficult than while at home where you control your food. It is possible, however, with some additional thought and planning to maintain your low carb lifestyle. The degree of difficulty will vary, whether you are traveling in your own recreational vehicle, driving and staying in hotels, flying and staying in hotels, or staying with friends. We provide you with travel tips to deal with each situation.

Recreation Vehicle

A vacation in your own recreational vehicle, whether it is a large motor home or a small tent trailer, will be the easiest type of travel to control your food intake. Although in this situation you may want to eat out on occasion, you are generally responsible for the preparation of meals. It means some modification to the usual outdoor cooking we associate with vacations. You will need to put a little thought into your grocery shopping and your meals. You may want to do hamburgers. Go ahead and have hamburgers, as long as there is no hamburger bun involved. We have gotten into the habit of having our burger patties, with or without cheese, with some fried onions and mushrooms and a nice big salad. This is a wonderful meal. We haven't eaten many hotdogs since beginning our low carb lifestyle, but it can be done, as long as no bun is involved. Just don't pack the potato chips or nachos!

Bring extra salad makings, some coleslaw and other raw vegetables for snacks and to fill in the meals. Bring extra low carb fruits to have on hand for snacks or desserts while camping. Have bacon and eggs for breakfast, or bake Patricia's home made low carb bars or muffins and pack them with you. (You will find the recipes for these in Chapter 8, New and Amazing Recipes.) If you really want to have something outside your normal meal plan because you are on vacation it is entirely up to you. We caution you however, that if you eat high carb at every meal or have an ice cream cone a day, you will gain weight. If vacation means vacation from your low carb plan, as well as your work, you will suffer the consequences.

Flying

If you are flying and the flight is a short one, food is not a big concern. If you are on an eight hour flight, you will need to eat on the plane. You can hope that the meal served on board has sufficient low carb food, or you can be proactive and plan your meal. In our experience, most in-flight meals are full of bread, cakes, cookies and sandwiches. If the airline is serving a dinner that includes a chicken breast with vegetables and a small salad, you can ignore the bread and dessert on the tray, and enjoy a healthy meal. Another option is to request a 'special meal'. Most airlines allow passengers with special dietary needs to order meals to meet their needs. There are many options available from vegetarian, to gluten free (no wheat products) or vegan (no dairy, no meat, no eggs). We find that most of these lack flavor and imagination, but we sometimes eat them.

Another option, and the one we are most likely to employ for ourselves, is to pack some snack foods in our carry on luggage and feed ourselves! We may pack a couple of low carb bars (either commercial or home made), some almonds and some cheese. Unless we are in the air all day long, this will be sufficient. We always take advantage of the available drinks in flight, and keep ourselves hydrated with bottled water, soda water, tea and diet drinks. These go a long way towards filling up your stomach with the aid of the snack foods.

Driving

Traveling by car and staying in hotels can be done with relative ease. If you are on the road for a couple of days to get to a vacation destination, there are some things you can do to make it easier on yourself. We always carry the protein powder from one of the commercial, low carb protein shakes with us. (Please see Chapter 10 on Low Carb Products and Resources to learn more about these.) We also carry a small plastic cup that has a tight rubber lid. Just mix a little powder with some water, shake well and voila! You now have a chocolate or strawberry protein shake for breakfast. The advantages of this approach are many. You don't have to leave your hotel room to find breakfast. The time to prepare and consume the shake probably takes no more than 3 to 5 minutes. And, you have just had a breakfast of approximately 2-3 grams of carb. This is a great way to start your day. Most hotel and motel rooms now provide the means for you to make a cup of instant coffee or tea, so you can have a complete breakfast without leaving your room.

If you prefer to have bacon and eggs, find yourself a nearby restaurant. Good options on the road are Denny's or International House of Pancakes (IHOP). We always ask for our bacon and eggs, or sausage and eggs to be served without the potato and bread. We find it easier to eat our breakfast without having to leave food on the plate (which is wasteful). This strategy also ensures we aren't tempted by something we might want to sample.

Lunch on the road may be slightly more difficult than dinner. When we travel by car, we almost always want lunch to be a quick stop and then continue on our way. We usually stop for the night and find a motel before we eat dinner, so there is no rush involved, and we ask the motel staff for recommendations. We have developed some strategies for lunch on the road that work well for us. If all we can find is fast food spots lining the highway, we will pick one that serves salads as an option. The best ones for this are Sizzlers, Subway, McDonalds or Wendys. The one that we prefer is Sizzlers. You can buy the 'All you can eat salad bar' and usually fill yourself up on healthy low carb foods. Subway is also easy. They now have salads that are made as you watch, and you instruct them concerning exactly what you would like to have. Patricia usually has lots of lettuce with green peppers and cucumber, and a warm sliced chicken breast on top. This is quite a good low carb, fast food lunch! In McDonalds we often order the chicken nuggets and a side salad. Another option is to find a restaurant like Denny's and have an omelet for lunch with a side salad. This is a great option if you had the protein shake for breakfast.

Traveling by car also means that you need to think ahead to how many days you will be on the road and ensure that you have sufficient snacks available. Whenever we stop for gas or at a rest stop, we buy cold drinks to keep in the car. We normally buy bottled water, or soda water. Diet drinks are also a good option as long as you recognize that there is aspartame in most diet drinks. We carry nuts in zip lock bags and low carb protein bars to use as snacks while we drive. We also have sugar free hard candies, mints and sugar free gum. Again, it means a little bit of extra thought and some additional organization, but this will contribute towards making your trip more pleasant and worry free. It will also allow you to travel without fear of putting on the weight you have lost.

Another small tip about traveling and staying in hotels concerns how to manage your weekly weigh-ins. If your trip is only a week or two in duration, this will not be a major concern. If, on the other hand, you are away for four weeks or more, you will want to weigh yourself to ensure that you are staying on the right track. We find a department store and go to the bathroom section. Find a bathroom scale that has been taken out of its packaging, put it on the floor and step up! We have done this more than once, just to check.

Visiting Friends

Staying with friends while you are on vacation can be a little more difficult than staying in hotels where you can choose your foods from a restaurant menu. The same as going to dinner at the home of friends, we always provide some advance notice of our dietary peculiarities so our friends are not caught off guard. It is much easier to plan meals for visitors if you know, for example, that they do not eat bread or potatoes. We always tell our friends that they should feel free to serve bread and potatoes if that is their normal habit, but to delete these items from our plates. We are always trying to maintain our low carb lifestyle while keeping it relatively easy for friends to have us as visitors.

It can be a bit of a difficult juggling act for us sometimes. We usually travel with our protein powder so if our friends have only cold cereal for breakfast, we just make a protein shake and everyone is happy. Cooked oatmeal can be an option for breakfast on an occasional basis. If we are staying with friends for a few days it is our experience that they will adapt quickly to our dietary needs. Patricia often offers to help with the cooking or to cook a couple of low carb meals while we visit. Most of our friends enjoy this very much and it helps us control our food intake.

Enjoying the Holidays

Holiday time can be stressful. During Thanksgiving, Hanukkah or Christmas there is a tendency to do things in extreme. We tend to party too much, eat too much, and spend too much during the holidays. How many people do you know who count on putting weight on during the holidays, and 'diet' every year when the holidays are finished? Many of us worry about money at holiday time, and the fear of putting on weight adds to our stress. Maintaining your low carb approach to eating during the holidays can be accomplished. As when we are vacationing, it simply takes some thought and a little discipline.

We recently had a very powerful example of both the right and the wrong way to approach the holidays. We were home in Victoria for the holidays, and had a number of invitations to Christmas parties and get togethers. We wanted to see all our friends and celebrate the season with them, so off we went. All of these social events involved food. The trick is to think through, in advance of the event, how you are going to approach your eating.

If a buffet is served that involves either appetizer type food or a full meal, it is usually easy to find enough food of the low carb variety to fill your hunger. If you are worried about it, have a low carb snack before leaving home. This can be particularly helpful if only appetizers are served and you are worried that the party may run past your normal dinner hour. When we attended the parties over the holidays, Patricia was quite strict with her food, finding lots of raw vegetables, stuffed mushrooms, nuts and other low carb appetizers. Harv, on the other hand, chose not to resist the small pastries, sausage rolls, samosas, egg rolls, bread and chip dips.

The same principle applies to a buffet dinner. It is easy to pick and choose from the food that is offered, to ensure that your meal stays relatively low carb. You will almost always find some low carb vegetables and a variety of salads. Load up on these foods so that your plate doesn't look empty and you have a pleasant meal. A caution about salads is to look closely at the contents before deciding what is appropriate for you. Salads often have hidden ingredients that can sabotage your meal, such as raisins or marshmallows. This is especially true during the holidays, when everyone wants food to look particularly attractive and taste yummy!

Perhaps the biggest challenge during the holidays will be to resist all the great desserts. We both had to struggle somewhat with this, as home made candy and chocolates, as well as shortbread cookies and other goodies have long been a tradition in our home. Not any more! Instead we had lots of wonderful fresh fruit available in our home, we found some no sugar added chocolates (details to follow) and Patricia developed a low carb Raspberry Cheesecake (see Chapter 8, New & Amazing Recipes) to serve to guests in our home over the holidays.

Another strategy for going out to friends over the holidays, or any time of the year, is to volunteer to bring a dish. Patricia particularly likes to offer to bring dessert. We both still enjoy dessert after a meal, and Patricia has developed a number of low carb options that taste delicious. No one ever suspects that the great cake or crème brulé that they are eating is low carb food. A recent Christmas dinner was held at our daughter and son-in-law's home. We went early so Patricia could help with the preparations for the turkey dinner. Patricia had volunteered to bake and bring dessert. The result was that we had two wonderful options to choose from, and everyone was happy. For Christmas dinner we chose to eat the turkey with some low carb cranberry sauce, a little gravy and lots of vegetables. We did not eat the potato, sweet potato, or the dressing. We didn't feel deprived, and we ate until we were pleasantly full. It was interesting to note that when we were done eating we felt fine, satisfied but not uncomfortable. Other members of the family complained about being 'stuffed'.

These strategies can apply to many circumstances. You can choose to ignore your low carb approach to food, and splurge. It is the holiday season, after all, and a time to celebrate! You will have to deal with the consequences of this decision when the holidays are over. You can choose to stick to your low carb approach to food, and feel sorry for yourself or think of yourself as deprived of the fun of holiday foods. This will decrease your own enjoyment, and possibly the pleasure and fun of others in your family. Or, you can choose to accept your new eating habits, concentrate on the foods that you can eat, prepare treats that you can enjoy, and have a joyous and wonderful holiday season. As with most other options, the decisions are entirely up to you and you will be the person most directly impacted by the results.

Earlier in this section we remarked that we had experienced directly how best to approach the holidays, and what the consequences might be. Remember that Harv decided that he didn't want to resist the pastries and the sweets at the parties we attended? He certainly enjoyed himself at these events, but he put on 6 pounds over a couple of weeks just before Christmas! He was surprised at how quickly the carbs added up and how easily the weight piled on. Patricia attended the same parties, and enjoyed herself while sticking closely to her low carb plan. The result was that she didn't put on a single pound over the holidays. Harv had to be very strict with his food for the two weeks following the holidays, and in that time he dropped the weight he had gained. If you are prepared to do this extra work then feel free to splurge. If, like Patricia, you prefer to maintain a very steady weight, you just need to be a little more disciplined with your food.

As we have mentioned, we are both non-drinkers of alcohol by choice. This is another area that you may want to think about in advance of the holidays and the associated social gatherings. We always take a large bottle of soda water with us when we go out to friends. We leave the bottle in the car until we determine that there is only fruit punch, mulled wine or eggnog available for drinks. At this point we go to the car and bring in our soda water. We used to love eggnog at Christmas (without any rum), but it is very high in carbs and we decided it will no longer be one of our choices. Mulled wine or hot mulled cider is also likely to be very high in carbs and fruit punch is always high due to the fruit juices. It all comes down to choices. The strategies that we have outlined for dealing with the holidays apply equally well to any party or celebration. As with most other things in life, if you think through the possibilities and plan for options that suit your needs, you will have fun and so will the people around you.

Educate Yourself

The best defense against making errors in judgment about foods or food products is to educate (or maybe re-educate) yourself. Reading this book is a great way to start. We read voraciously. We read everything we can find that relates to low carb or nutrition or food. We read books, newspaper articles, magazine articles, medical reviews and research articles, and information available on the web. Most of you will not have the time, the energy or the desire to go to the lengths that we have. That's probably why you bought this book, and it is certainly one of our motivations in writing it. We want to distill the important findings and present them in a manner that makes it easy for you to understand.

What you can do, and should do, is to start reading labels on foods and food products. Remember when the whole idea of low fat first emerged, before all the new low fat products were available? There was always someone in the aisle of the grocery store pouring over the small type on the label. We want you to become one of these people, especially when you first start your low carb plan. Take time with your shopping, and read the labels. We have already identified some of the products that surprised us when we started eating this way. A simple example is commercial salad dressings. The low fat dressings have added sugar for flavor, so they are very high in carbohydrates. The regular salad dressings do not have the added sugar so the carb content drops considerably. Read all of the dressing labels until you find one or two that appeal to your palate, and have a low carb content. We find the vinaigrette dressings often have only a couple of grams of carb in each tablespoon. There are also creamy dressings that are very low in carb, you just have to stand in the aisle reading labels until you find one that you like. We often make our own dressings, from recipes in *Easy Low Carb Cooking*, or with simple oil and vinegar combinations. We also like to have prepared dressings on hand for those times when food preparation is rushed.

An important point to remember is that we need to pay attention to the serving size for which the nutrition information is being given. One tablespoon of salad dressing will often be enough for us, as we don't like to 'drown' our salads. If, however, you like a lot of dressing on your salad, you need to consider this in the calculation of your carb count. You may find that you will need to cut down on the amount of dressing you use if it has increased the number of grams of carb you consume in a day.

Patricia haunts the diabetic aisles of every new grocery store she enters. She is always looking for new foods or products that have little or no sugar and can become part of our low carb plan. The possibilities are endless, as more and more manufacturers are catering both to the diabetic population, and the 'low carbers' of the world. We have found low sugar diabetic chocolates, low sugar diabetic jams and jellies, sugar free hard candy, sugar free mints and gum, and a host of other products. We also note that more and more products are being developed especially for low carb diets. We think this is wonderful! Look at the influence this approach has had on the market place. We have dedicated Chapter 10 of this book to an overview of these products and our experience in using them.

Have Faith & Go Easy on Yourself

If you make a bad food choice, don't give up. It's not the end of the world. If you completely 'fall off the wagon' and binge on Pizza or some other high carb food, you have not ruined anything. Just get right back up on that wagon! We are advocating a change in the way you live your life. It will take a while for you to get accustomed to this change. Don't dwell on your slips or mistakes; think about all the positive steps you have taken. If you make a choice to eat some high carb foods and want to do something about it, go for a walk or involve yourself in some other form of physical activity. This will have a two fold benefit. It will take your mind off the mistake, and it will increase your metabolic rate to help burn off those carbs. Forgive yourself and vow to try harder. Then throw any left over Pizza in the garbage and dispose of it. Who needs that kind of temptation? This is a life long strategy. We all have days that are easier than others. Go easy on yourself if you slip up, and have faith that the low carb plan will work for you.

We hope that this chapter will assist you in recognizing the various options that are available to us all, to help maintain our new healthy lifestyle. All of the situations or suggestions in this chapter come from our own experience of trial and error, and the experiences of our friends and family. It took us a considerable time to make the switch in our thinking when we decided to eat low carb. It is our hope that these strategies will ease the transition for you. We have a number of helpful suggestions to make about food preparation and how to keep things quick and simple that we present in the following chapter.

Our strategies for success include:

♦ Planning your meals
♦ Eating more frequently and eating smaller amounts
♦ Eating smart in restaurants and at friends'
♦ Traveling without stress
♦ Enjoying special holidays
♦ Educating yourself
♦ Forgiving yourself

CHAPTER 7

Menu Planning

"Marketing once a week – with a full menu plan in hand – is a wonderful way to control what you eat."
Dr. Rachel F. Heller and Dr. Richard F. Heller

Perhaps the most difficult thing for beginners embarking on a low carb food plan is how to plan meals that will be tasty and nutritious as well as low carb. We will take away the worry and concern about this issue. We have developed a week of daily menus for low carb weight loss as well as a week of menus for low carb maintenance. We have also provided some menu ideas for entertaining, to make this easier for you. We don't intend that these are the only foods that you should eat, but it will remove the mystery for you to see how we have approached this task. If you want to follow these menu plans exactly, it will provide a good start for either phase of low carb living.

This chapter contains a number of tips regarding how to simplify things in the kitchen to make meal preparation quick and easy. We share the things that have worked best in our household. Ensuring that low carb foods are always readily available will reduce waste and minimize the time spent in the kitchen. Even good cooks like Patricia don't want to spend all their time in the kitchen and occasionally want to put together a really quick and easy meal. We have also included a list of low carb snack foods to make things easier for you. Pick the snacks that appeal to you.

All of the recipes in Menu Planning are found either in Patricia's cookbook, *Easy Low Carb Cooking*, or are contained in the chapter following this one. The exceptions are simple items like 'steamed broccoli'.

We have made the assumption that you don't need a recipe to tell you how to steam fresh vegetables. All of the recipes in both the cookbook and this book start with the freshest, best quality foods and ingredients available to us. We don't use frozen vegetables – ever! Not only is there a considerable loss of nutrients in frozen vegetables, but they don't taste as good and are not as pleasing to the eye. Taste, smell and appearance are all important when starting a low carb plan.

This basic principle applies to the purchase of all ingredients. When we buy olive oil, we buy the very best extra virgin olive oil we can afford. We particularly like the 'light' olive oils that have a paler color and light flavor. When we buy vinegar for cooking or salad dressings, we buy the best red wine or balsamic vinegar we can find. This is a good general rule to follow, while keeping your food budget in mind. We want to make eating low carb a pleasant experience, as well as a healthy one. You will find that Patricia has a number of suggestions about presentation of foods in her cookbook, to increase your pleasure in eating them.

> *"I have been using the cookbook (Everyday Low Carb Cooking*) for about a month now. I keep it out on the kitchen counter always. The recipes are fabulous and easy and help me to renew my old way of cooking with Patricia's fresh and healthy ideas. I'm impressing my friends with the new recipes and they are raving about how good they taste. It's like having a good friend with me in the kitchen."*
> Annette Wall, Victoria, British Columbia, Canada

*Now available under the title, Easy Low Carb Cooking.

Please note that we have provided some menus for entertaining, just to get you started. When we have friends in for dinner, they always enjoy the food, even though it is all low carb! You will notice that some of the low carb desserts are a little higher in carb content than others. Patricia likes to serve wonderful desserts. We are very careful when we entertain to control our carb intake for a day or two before and after a dinner party, so that there is no adverse effect on our weight or our health.

Snack Foods

Many people wonder what foods are appropriate as snacks on a low carbohydrate diet. The following list will provide some ideas. Snacks should be kept to less than 3 grams of carbohydrates, whenever possible. Although we list low carb bars as an acceptable snack, there is new information about the labeling and carb content of these products that causes us some concern. Please review the section dealing with low carb bars in Chapter 10 on Low Carb Products and Resources carefully, before making a decision about these products and whether to introduce them into your food plan.

- low carb bar of choice (see Low Carb Products, Chapter 10 for details)
- home made low carb bar (see New & Amazing Recipes, Chapter 8 for details)
- low carb muffins (see New & Amazing Recipes, Chapter 8 for details)
- 8 oz. protein shake (see Low Carb Products, Chapter 10 for details)
- 12 oz. Fresca or other diet drink (contains aspartame)
- 1 stick of string cheese
- 1 oz. any cheese
- 1 hard boiled egg
- 1 deviled egg
- 1 poached egg
- ½ cucumber, cut into fingers, with fresh lemon or lime juice
- 1 medium celery stick filled with 1 tablespoon of cream cheese
- 1 medium celery stick filled with 1 tablespoon of peanut butter
- ¼ cup dry curd or 4% fat cottage cheese (the dry curds have the lowest carb content)
- ¼ cup of whole plain yogurt
- 1 small slice of cooked ham or turkey
- ham & cheese roll-up (see New & Amazing Recipes, Chapter 8 for details)
- sugar free jello
- (8-10) cashews or almonds (a small fist full)
- ½ cup pork rinds
- sugar free gum or mints
- herb tea

Grocery List

For readers who are completely new to the idea of a low carb kitchen and the ingredients necessary to prepare low carb meals, we have developed a very typical week's worth of groceries. The list varies from week to week and our actual menu plan, but here are some basics. Some of the staples you will need in a low carb kitchen, such as regular mayonnaise, are included to help you reorganize your kitchen supplies. You may not need all these ingredients, and you may not need them all at once, but this will provide a place to start when making your own list.

- eggs
- light cream
- heavy cream
- plain yogurt
- cottage cheese
- cheddar cheese
- balsamic vinegar
- olive oil
- ½ pound of butter
- head of lettuce
- bag of mixed wild greens
- 2 cucumbers
- celery
- cauliflower
- green beans
- asparagus
- zucchini
- green cabbage
- red cabbage
- green onion
- onion
- mushrooms
- 2 carrots
- green pepper
- real mayonnaise
- 2 lemons
- lemon juice
- 2 limes

- small container of fresh strawberries, if available
- kiwi fruit, if available
- bacon
- boneless and skinless chicken breasts – lots!
- lean ground beef
- fresh fish
- sugar free jello, many flavors
- soda water
- herb tea
- coffee
- decaff coffee
- Fresca or other diet drink, if desired (contains aspartame)
- canned tuna

Shortcuts

This section is a compilation of food preparation tips to make your time in the kitchen easier and more enjoyable. Through years of being a busy working step-mom, and after over two years of low carbohydrate food preparation, Patricia has developed a number of strategies and shortcuts to make meal preparation quick and easy. Not every recipe in her cookbook lends itself to the type of time saving tips that are presented here, but many of them will work well using these guidelines.

We mentioned earlier that we like to buy fresh meats, poultry, fish and vegetables, and we do. We also prefer to buy groceries once weekly, and plan our food consumption around what is available. This means that although we try to use much of it while fresh, we do freeze some of our meat and poultry. We almost never freeze our fish, preferring to cook it fresh. We buy poultry and meat in large quantities to get the best price. When we come home with groceries, we take the time to divide the poultry and meat into appropriate serving sizes, wrap in plastic wrap and then put them into freezer bags. This method ensures that no frost or freezer burn occurs in the food. It also means these freezer bags can be reused many times because no meat or poultry actually touches the inside of the bag. We usually freeze four boneless and skinless chicken breasts to a package. We normally cook all four together and eat two immediately and the rest sometime later. The same is true of the meat portions we freeze.

Sometimes rather than freezing the chicken or meat as above, we put them directly into a zip-lock bag and add marinade. Give the bag a shake or two and then freeze. The poultry or meat will tenderize and flavor while it thaws and will be ready to cook when you get home later in the day. If you are using Patricia's marinade recipes, you will want to substitute dried herbs (instead of the fresh herbs found in her recipes) when freezing.

We always have bacon available at home, but don't necessarily eat a full package right away. We separate the bacon into small packages of 2 or 4 slices and wrap them individually and put a bunch of these packages in freezer bags to freeze. This way, we always have appropriate servings available for breakfast, in omelets or to crumble over a salad.

When we have extra poultry or meat left at the end of a meal we sometimes divide it into individual portions and either cube or slice it very thinly. We freeze this cooked protein and it is ready to pull out for a quick snack. It is also ready to add to a salad or to a few cooked vegetables (done in the microwave if you like) for a really quick and easy meal. This is also a good way to start Patricia's Chicken Wraps! (See Chapter 8, New & Amazing Recipes.)

We often make a big batch of Patricia's Spicy Chicken Wings and eat as many as we like with salad as a meal. The left overs can be frozen in individual freezer bags and thawed and reheated for a quick snack as is, or another quick meal with a green salad.

On a night when we are feeling really lazy, or have not had time to do anything about dinner, we buy a rotisserie (BBQ'd) chicken at the store and bring it home. Simply add a big green salad and dinner is served! This makes a great no fuss meal. We often make a chicken salad the next day and freeze any left over chicken to use for soups, salads or other quick meal. Save the carcass, and freeze it.

When you have 3 or 4 small carcasses you can make chicken stock. Put the carcass in a large soup pot, add water, large chunks of onion, celery tops with the leaves still on, carrot, dried herbs, and salt and pepper. Let this simmer for 3-4 hours (or all day) on the stove and then strain. You now have wonderful fragrant and tasty chicken broth.

Beef stock can be made with beef bones the same way as chicken stock is made. These stocks can be used as the base for homemade soups or in sauces. Beef or chicken stock can be frozen, to pull out when you need it. A good way to freeze these liquids is in small individual containers. A single serving of stock can be the basis for a quick lunch, with the addition of a small green salad.

When we bake or poach salmon, we always make extra. The next day we enjoy salmon salad or cold salmon with green salad.

Egg whites freeze well. When Patricia makes either her Crème Framboise (see *Easy Low Carb Cooking*), or her French Cream desserts (which call for 4 egg yolks each) she freezes the whites, two to a freezer bag. These are available anytime for an omelet, scrambled eggs or other dish.

Use thinly sliced zucchini or eggplant in place of noodles for lasagna.

Use cooked spaghetti squash instead of pasta and cover with your favorite tomato or meat sauce.

Use thinly sliced, cooked green cabbage in place of either noodles or rice. Pour your favorite curry dish or spaghetti sauce over the cabbage and enjoy guilt free!

Shredded zucchini can be used as a low carb filler in many dishes, including meat loaf or cabbage rolls (see Patricia's recipe in the New & Amazing Recipes, Chapter 8). Zucchini is very mild in flavor, and will not overpower the rest of the dish if used appropriately. We have even used it in our new muffins.

Experiment on your own to find additional quick and easy low carb meals and alternatives. Once you become familiar with the best low carb vegetables and other ingredients, you can adjust your own favorite family recipes and enjoy them. We welcome your ideas at our website, www.lowcarbliving.ca, where we have devoted an entire section to recipe ideas, exchanges, and award winning recipes.

Breakfast Alternatives

One of the most frequently asked questions about the low carb meal plan is, "What do you do about breakfast?" This can be a challenge, especially if you get tired of bacon and eggs as regular fare. We have presented a number of options below, as either appropriate for low carb weight loss or low carb maintenance. Most of the alternatives are relatively 'normal' breakfast foods. You can always opt for the unusual, as long as you keep track of the carbohydrate content of the foods.

As mentioned earlier, we don't recommend you skip breakfast. It is important to start your day with a nourishing meal. In fact, Drs. Eades in *The Protein Power Lifeplan* explain, "Studies have shown that what you (or your kids) eat for breakfast sets the tone of what you (or they) will want to eat at the end of the day. Recent studies have proven that a higher-protein, higher-fat breakfast, lower in sugars and starches, will prevent overeating later on and may be a big factor in preventing the rising epidemic of childhood and adolescent obesity, a problem that has doubled in the last ten years!" (p.361)

Breakfast Alternatives Suitable for Weight Loss

Breakfast Option		Grams of Carb
Bacon & eggs *		1.2
Sausage & eggs*		1.2
Ham & eggs*		1.2
½ cup dry curd cottage cheese		2.0
with ¼ cup sliced strawberries	2.6	4.6
½ cup whole plain yogurt		5.0
with ¼ cup toasted seeds and nuts	4.0	9.0
½ cup ricotta cheese		3.8
with ½ fresh chopped tomato	2.9	6.7
Low Carb Citrus Bar***		5.4
Low Carb Chocolate Nut Bar***		7.3
Magic Muffin***		7.8
Coconut Zucchini Muffins***		5.4
Lemon Carrot Muffins***		10.3
Strawberry Smoothie***		7.2
Mushroom & Cheese Omelet**		4.0
Mushroom & Spinach Frittata**		3.6
Smoked salmon, raw onion, capers & lemon juice		3.6
Low carb protein shake		2-3

* Eggs may be fried, scrambled, poached, or boiled.

** All recipes designated with ** can be found in Patricia's cookbook, *Easy Low Carb Cooking*.

*** All recipes designated with *** are found in Chapter 8, New & Amazing Recipes.

Breakfast Alternatives Suitable for Maintenance

Breakfast Option		Grams of Carb
Bowl of hot oatmeal *		16.0
With light cream		
Bowl of hot oatmeal		20.0
With 2-3 sliced strawberries		
½ fresh grapefruit		12.0
2 slices low carb bread		20.0
½ cup 4% fat cottage cheese		4.0
with ½ cup sliced strawberries	5.2	9.2
or ½ cup fresh raspberries	7.1	11.1
or ½ cup blackberries	9.2	13.2
or ½ cup blueberries	10.2	14.2
½ cup whole plain yogurt		5.0
with ½ cup sliced strawberries	5.2	10.2
or ½ cup fresh raspberries	7.1	12.1
or ½ cup blackberries	9.2	14.2
or ½ cup blueberries	10.2	15.2
Small Spinach Salad		8.0

* When making your oatmeal, be sure to use regular oats that take 3 to 4 minutes to cook, and *not* the instant variety. The chemical process that is used to make the oats 'instant' dramatically changes the glycemic index. While regular oats have a low glycemic index, the instant variety have a high glycemic index and are therefore not recommended. The grams of carbohydrate were calculated based on 1/3 cup of the raw oats, as per manufacturer's labeling. You may want to add some Splenda to sweeten your oatmeal or a little cinnamon or nutmeg.

We hope that these suggestions and ideas will help you add variety and interest to your breakfasts. All of the above breakfast ideas may be enjoyed with tea or decaff coffee and a glass of water (or fruit flavored Crystal Light, keeping in mind that it contains aspartame). You may use any of the weight loss breakfast options during maintenance as well.

We would be delighted to receive your creative breakfast ideas, or other low carb food ideas, at our website www.lowcarbliving.ca.

Menu Planning – Weight Loss

Here are menus for seven days of meals that are suitable for low carb weight loss. All of the daily menus have been developed to maintain a carbohydrate content of less than 30 grams a day.

Recipes designated with ** indicate they can be found in Patricia's cookbook, *Easy Low Carb Cooking*. Recipes designated with *** are in Chapter 8, New & Amazing Recipes.

MENU PLANNING   WEIGHT LOSS
Day One

		Carbohydrates
Breakfast	2 eggs, scrambled	1.2
	2 slices of bacon	0.0
	coffee, light cream	0.5
Snack	1 oz. cheddar cheese	0.4
	decaff coffee, light cream	0.5
Lunch	Tuna Salad**	2.4
	green salad (1 tbsp vinaigrette)	3.0
	sugar free jello	0.0
	water, herb tea	0.0
Snack	1/2 cucumber, lemon juice	1.4
	herb tea	0.0
Dinner	Grilled Herb Chicken**	2.3
	Grilled Zucchini**	3.4
	Asparagus with Balsamic Vinegar**	5.8
	green salad (1 tbsp vinaigrette)	3.0
	1/2 C. sliced strawberries	5.2
	water, herb tea	0.0
	Total Carbohydrates	**29.1**

Crystal Light fruit drink may be added to any breakfast. Be aware that it contains aspartame.

Recipes designated with ** indicate they can be found in Patricia's cookbook, *Easy Low Carb Cooking*. Recipes designated with *** are in Chapter 8, New & Amazing Recipes.

MENU PLANNING   WEIGHT LOSS
Day Two

		Carbohydrates
Breakfast	1/2 C. cottage cheese	2.0
	1/4 C. sliced strawberries	2.6
	coffee, light cream	0.5
Snack	1/2 low carb bar*	1.0
	decaff coffee, light cream	0.5
Lunch	Chicken Salad**	4.0
	green salad (1 tbsp vinaigrette)	3.0
	sugar free jello	0.0
	water, herb tea	0.0
Snack	8-10 almonds	2.5
	herb tea	0.0
Dinner	Salmon Poached in White Wine**	2.7
	1/2 C. steamed cauliflower	2.6
	Green Beans with Mustard**	1.1
	Easy Coleslaw**	3.4
	sugar free jello	0.0
	water, herb tea	0.0
	Total Carbohydrates	**25.9**

* We don't recommend you eat low carb bars too frequently, particularly during weight loss.

Recipes designated with ** indicate they can be found in Patricia's cookbook, *Easy Low Carb Cooking*. Recipes designated with *** are in Chapter 8, New & Amazing Recipes.

MENU PLANNING   WEIGHT LOSS
Day Three

		Carbohydrates
Breakfast	2 eggs, poached	2.0
	1 slice ham	0.0
	coffee, light cream	0.5
Snack	Ham & Cheese Roll-Up***	1.7
	decaff coffee, light cream	0.5
Lunch	Salmon Salad**	2.6
	1/2 C. red lettuce	2.0
	1/2 C. cucumber slices	1.0
	sugar free jello	0.0
	water, herb tea	0.0
Snack	1/2 C. pork rinds	0.0
	Fresca*	0.0
Dinner	Teriyaki Burger**	1.9
	1/2 C. steamed broccoli	4.0
	Grilled Eggplant***	8.3
	Easy Coleslaw**	3.4
	sugar free jello	0.0
	water, herb tea	0.0
	Total Carbohydrates	**27.9**

* This drink contains aspartame.

Recipes designated with ** indicate they can be found in Patricia's cookbook, *Easy Low Carb Cooking*. Recipes designated with *** are in Chapter 8, New & Amazing Recipes.

	MENU PLANNING	**WEIGHT LOSS**
Day Four		
		Carbohydrates
Breakfast	1/2 C. whole plain yogurt	5.0
	1/4 C. sliced strawberries	2.6
	coffee, light cream	0.5
Snack	1 hard boiled egg	1.0
	decaff coffee, light cream	0.5
Lunch	Cold Teriyaki Burger**	1.9
	Easy Coleslaw**	3.4
	1/4 C. sliced strawberries	2.6
	water, herb tea	0.0
Snack	8-10 almonds	2.5
	herb tea	0.0
Dinner	Roast Chicken with Lemon & Rosemary**	0.5
	1/2 C. steamed asparagus	2.5
	Creamy Garlic Cauliflower**	3.5
	green salad (1 tbsp vinaigrette)	3.0
	sugar free jello	0.0
	water, herb tea	0.0
	Total Carbohydrates	**29.5**

Recipes designated with ** indicate they can be found in Patricia's cookbook, *Easy Low Carb Cooking*. Recipes designated with *** are in Chapter 8, New & Amazing Recipes.

MENU PLANNING	**WEIGHT LOSS**
Day Five	
	Carbohydrates

Breakfast	Mushroom & Spinach Frittata**	3.6
	coffee, light cream	0.5
Snack	1 celery stick,1 tbsp. cream cheese	1.5
	decaff coffee, light cream	0.5
Lunch	Spinach Salad**	8.0
	sugar free jello	0.0
	water, herb tea	0.0
Snack	1/2 low carb bar	1.0
	Fresca*	0.0
Dinner	cold chicken	0.0
	Spicy Oven Baked Zucchini**	3.4
	Green Beans with Onions & Vinegar**	3.6
	green salad (1 tbsp vinaigrette)	3.0
	1/4 C. sliced strawberries	2.6
	water, herb tea	0.0
	Total Carbohydrates	**27.7**

* This drink contains aspartame.

Recipes designated with ** indicate they can be found in Patricia's cookbook, *Easy Low Carb Cooking*. Recipes designated with *** are in Chapter 8, New & Amazing Recipes.

MENU PLANNING   WEIGHT LOSS
Day Six

Carbohydrates

Breakfast	1/2 C. cottage cheese	2.0
	1/4 C. sliced strawberries	2.6
	coffee, light cream	0.5
Snack	1 celery stick, 1 tbsp. peanut butter	4.0
	decaff coffee, light cream	0.5
Lunch	Mushroom & Spinach Frittata**	3.6
	green salad (1 tbsp vinaigrette)	3.0
	sugar free jello	0.0
	water, herb tea	0.0
Snack	1/2 cup pork rinds	0.0
	herb tea	0.0
Dinner	Steamed Halibut with	
	Herbs & Vegetables**	7.4
	1/2 C. steamed green beans	4.0
	green salad (1 tbsp vinaigrette)	3.0
	sugar free jello	0.0
	water, herb tea	0.0
	Total Carbohydrates	**30.6**

Recipes designated with ** indicate they can be found in Patricia's cookbook, *Easy Low Carb Cooking*. Recipes designated with *** are in Chapter 8, New & Amazing Recipes.

MENU PLANNING	**WEIGHT LOSS**
Day Seven	
	Carbohydrates

Breakfast	Strawberry Smoothie***	4.6
	coffee, light cream	0.5
Snack	1 hard boiled egg	0.0
	decaff coffee, light cream	0.5
Lunch	Waldorf Salad**	11.5
	sugar free jello	0.0
	water, herb tea	0.0
Snack	1 oz. cheddar cheese	0.4
	herb tea	0.0
Dinner	Peppered Steak**	0.7
	Broccoli Supreme**	3.3
	1/2 C. steamed cauliflower	2.9
	Tangy Coleslaw**	2.6
	1/4 C. sliced strawberries	2.6
	water, herb tea	0.0
	Total Carbohydrates	**29.6**

Note: This Smoothie is made with just 1/4 cup of berries.

Menu Planning – Maintenance

We have prepared seven days of menu plans that are suitable for low carb maintenance. The total grams of carbohydrate vary between 35 and 50 grams a day.

Recipes designated with ** indicate they can be found in Patricia's cookbook, *Easy Low Carb Cooking*. Recipes designated with *** are in Chapter 8, New & Amazing Recipes.

MENU PLANNING   MAINTENANCE
Day One

		Carbohydrates
Breakfast	oatmeal, light cream	16.0
	coffee, light cream	0.5
Snack	Ham & Cheese Roll-Up***	1.7
	decaff coffee, light cream	0.5
Lunch	Lemon Herb Chicken **	1.4
	green salad (1 tbsp vinaigrette)	3.0
	sugar free jello	0.0
	water, herb tea	0.0
Snack	1 oz. cheddar cheese	0.4
	herb tea	0.0
Dinner	Meatloaf**	4.1
	Creamy Garlic Cauliflower**	3.5
	1/4 C. steamed green beans	2.0
	green salad (1 tbsp vinaigrette)	3.0
	sugar free jello, whipped cream	1.0
	water, herb tea	0.0
	Total Carbohydrates	**37.1**

Recipes designated with ** indicate they can be found in Patricia's cookbook, *Easy Low Carb Cooking*. Recipes designated with *** are in Chapter New & Amazing Recipes.

	MENU PLANNING	MAINTENANCE
Day Two		
		Carbohydrates
Breakfast	Low Carb Citrus Bar***	5.4
	coffee, light cream	0.5
Snack	1 oz. cheddar cheese	0.4
	decaff coffee, light cream	0.5
Lunch	reheated meatloaf	4.1
	green salad (1 tbsp vinaigrette)	3.0
	1/2 C. sliced strawberries	5.2
	water, herb tea	0.0
Snack	1/2 cucumber, lemon juice	1.4
	herb tea	0.0
Dinner	Salmon Poached with Vegetables**	2.7
	Greens with Pecans & Blue Cheese**	6.6
	Strawberry Mousse**	5.9
	water, herb tea	0.0
	Total Carbohydrates	**35.7**

Recipes designated with ** indicate they can be found in Patricia's cookbook, *Easy Low Carb Cooking*. Recipes designated with *** are in Chapter 8, New & Amazing Recipes.

MENU PLANNING **Day Three**		MAINTENANCE
		Carbohydrates
Breakfast	1/2 C. cottage cheese	2.0
	1/2 C. fresh strawberries	5.2
	coffee, light cream	0.5
Snack	Ham & Cheese Roll-Up***	1.7
	decaff coffee, light cream	0.5
Lunch	Chicken Salad**	4.0
	Easy Coleslaw**	3.4
	water, herb tea	0.0
Snack	sugar free jello	0.0
	herb tea	0.0
Dinner	Steak with Roasted Vegetables**	17.8
	green salad (1 tbsp vinaigrette)	3.0
	sugar free jello	0.0
	water, herb tea	0.0
	Total Carbohydrates	**38.1**

Recipes designated with ** indicate they can be found in Patricia's cookbook, *Easy Low Carb Cooking*. Recipes designated with *** are in Chapter 8, New & Amazing Recipes.

MENU PLANNING   MAINTENANCE
Day Four

Carbohydrates

Breakfast	Mushroom & Cheese Omelet**	4.0
	2 slices of bacon	0.0
	coffee, light cream	0.5
Snack	1/2 Low Carb Citrus Bar***	2.7
	decaff coffee, light cream	0.5
Lunch	Spinach Salad**	8.0
	sugar free jello	0.0
	water, herb tea	0.0
Snack	8-10 almonds	2.5
	Fresca*	0.0
Dinner	Orange Chicken**	2.1
	1/2 C. steamed cauliflower	2.9
	1/2 C. steamed green beans	4.0
	green salad (1 tbsp vinaigrette)	3.0
	Quick & Easy Vanilla Mousse**	10.0
	water, herb tea	0.0
	Total Carbohydrates	**40.2**

* This drink contains aspartame.

Recipes designated with ** indicate they can be found in Patricia's cookbook, *Easy Low Carb Cooking*. Recipes designated with *** are in Chapter 8, New & Amazing Recipes.

	MENU PLANNING	**MAINTENANCE**
Day Five		
		Carbohydrates
Breakfast	oatmeal with light cream	16.0
	coffee, light cream	0.5
Snack	Ham & Cheese Roll-Up***	1.7
	decaff coffee, light cream	0.5
Lunch	Broccoli Soufflé**	6.6
	green salad (1 tbsp vinaigrette)	3.0
	water, herb tea	0.0
Snack	1/2 C. pork rinds	0.0
	Fresca*	0.0
Dinner	Turkey Burger**	6.4
	Grilled Asparagus**	5.4
	Grilled Zucchini**	3.4
	green salad (1 tbsp vinaigrette)	3.0
	sugar free jello	0.0
	water, herb tea	0.0
	Total Carbohydrates	**46.5**

* This drink contains aspartame.

Recipes designated with ** indicate they can be found in Patricia's cookbook, *Easy Low Carb Cooking*. Recipes designated with *** are in Chapter 8, New & Amazing Recipes.

MENU PLANNING		**MAINTENANCE**
Day Six		**Carbohydrates**
Breakfast	Magic Muffin***	7.8
	coffee, light cream	0.5
Snack	1/2 Low Carb Citrus Bar***	2.7
	decaff coffee, light cream	0.5
Lunch	Hearty Vegetable Soup***	10.9
	green salad (1 tbsp vinaigrette)	3.0
	water, herb tea	0.0
Snack	8-10 almonds	2.5
	Fresca*	0.0
Dinner	Crispy Oven Baked Chicken**	0.5
	Vegetable Medley**	8.2
	Fancy Coleslaw**	4.3
	1/2 C. sliced strawberries	5.2
	water, herb tea	0.0
	Total Carbohydrates	**46.1**

* This drink contains aspartame.

Recipes designated with ** indicate they can be found in Patricia's cookbook, *Easy Low Carb Cooking*. Recipes designated with *** are in Chapter 8, New & Amazing Recipes.

	MENU PLANNING	**MAINTENANCE**
Day Seven		
		Carbohydrates
Breakfast	2 eggs, scrambled	1.2
	2 slices of bacon	0.0
	coffee, light cream	0.5
Snack	Coconut Zucchini Muffin***	5.4
	decaff coffee, light cream	0.5
Lunch	French Onion Soup***	10.5
	green salad (1 tbsp vinaigrette)	3.0
	sugar free jello	0.0
	water, herb tea	0.0
Snack	1 stick celery, 1 tbsp cream cheese	1.5
	herb tea	0.0
Dinner	Broiled Halibut**	1.2
	Zucchini with Tomatoes**	9.4
	1/2 C. steamed asparagus	2.5
	green salad (1 tbsp vinaigrette)	3.0
	Cherry Compote**	2.3
	water, herb tea	0.0
	Total Carbohydrates	**41.0**

Menu Planning – Entertainment

We have presented some menu options to facilitate entertaining. You don't have to serve high carb foods to prepare delicious meals. Guests will enjoy these selections, and probably not even notice that they are eating low carb!

Recipes designated with ** indicate they can be found in Patricia's cookbook, *Easy Low Carb Cooking*. Recipes designated with *** are in Chapter 8, New & Amazing Recipes.

MENU PLANNING   ENTERTAINMENT

BRUNCH

	Carbohydrates
Mushroom & Spinach Frittata**	**3.6**
sliced smoked salmon or	0.0
sliced cold ham	0.0
Tangy Coleslaw**	2.9
1/2 C. sliced strawberries	5.2
decaff coffee, light cream	0.5
herb tea	0.0
Total Carbohydrates	**12.2**

LUNCH BUFFET*

Chicken Salad**	2.0
Cold Salmon with Dill Sauce**	1.6
Spinach Salad**	4.0
Broccoli Salad**	3.0
Crème Framboise**	6.4
tea	0.0
Total Carbohydrates	**17.0**

* The carb count has been reduced by 50% for each serving to accommodate a less than full portion.

DINNER
Option # 1

	Carbohydrates
Greens with Pecans & Blue Cheese**	5.9
Chicken with Citrus Cranberry Sauce**	4.7
steamed asparagus	2.5
Grilled Eggplant***	8.3
Raspberry Cheesecake***	9.5
tea, decaff coffee	0.5
Total Carbohydrates	**31.4**

DINNER
Option # 2

Creamy Broccoli Soup**	4.2
Rack of Lamb with Herbs & Spices**	2.4
Grilled Asparagus**	5.4
steamed cauliflower	2.6
Chocolate Indulgence**	13.8
tea, decaff coffee	0.0
Total Carbohydrates	**28.4**

DINNER
Option # 3

Summer Salad**	10.3
Baked Whole Salmon**	4.3
Green Beans with Bacon & Mushrooms**	9.3
steamed asparagus	2.5
Crème Framboise**	6.4
tea, decaff coffee	0.0
Total Carbohydrates	**32.8**

CHAPTER 8

New & Amazing Recipes

"Learn what chefs have known all along. A little bit of a high quality ingredient goes a long way toward boosting flavor."
Walter C. Willett, M.D.

This chapter offers some exciting new ideas that come as the result of experimentation. In her cookbook, Patricia made an effort to use everyday common ingredients in the recipes to make preparation quick and easy.

For her second book, Patricia wanted to develop low carb bars and muffins to broaden the scope of foods that we enjoy. In doing so, she has started to experiment with new and interesting ingredients like soy flour, oat flour, flax seed meal, protein isolate and other healthy alternatives. You will find these ingredients either in your local grocery store or a health food store. We have also included additional recipes that use everyday common ingredients. We're sure that you will enjoy these new foods.

All nutrition calculations have been made using the 'NutriBase 2001 Personal Plus' software. Every effort has been made to ensure the accuracy of the nutrition information.

Strawberry Smoothie

2 scoops strawberry flavored protein powder

½ cup frozen strawberries

¾ cup water

Nutrition Information Per Serving	
Calories	86.08
Protein	12.32 g.
Carbs	8.60 g.
Fat	0.08 g.

❃ Put all ingredients in a blender and blend until smooth.

Note: If you add just ¼ cup of the frozen berries, you cut your carb content to 5.4 grams total. This will be a somewhat 'thinner' smoothie. You may add other frozen berries to vary the flavor, but be aware of the carb content of each.

Coconut Zucchini Muffins

½ cup ground almonds

¼ cup each, ground sesame & sunflower seeds

½ cup flax meal

¼ cup soy flour

2 packets Splenda

½ teaspoon baking soda

½ teaspoon baking powder

½ teaspoon xanthan gum

¼ teaspoon salt

¼ cup sweetened coconut

1 egg, beaten

2 tablespoons olive oil

½ teaspoon coconut extract

¼ cup water

1 cup finely shredded zucchini (1 medium)

Nutrition Information Per Serving	
Calories	162.08
Protein	6.01 g.
Carbs	5.43 g.
Fat	13.85 g.

- ❀ Preheat oven to 375°.
- ❀ The nuts and seeds may be ground in a food processor.
- ❀ Mix all dry ingredients together. Mix wet ingredients in a separate bowl.
- ❀ Add wet ingredients to dry and stir to blend. Pour into muffin tins that have been lined with paper muffin cups.
- ❀ Bake for 25 minutes, until brown around the edges.
- ❀ Makes 8 muffins.

Variation: You can substitute pumkin seeds for the sesame seeds for a variation.
Note: Many thanks to my sister Stephanie Tompkins for developing this recipe.

Ham & Cheese Roll-Up

Nutrition Information Per Serving	
Calories	208.0
Protein	11.54 g.
Carbs	1.77 g.
Fat	17.25 g.

1 leaf green lettuce

1 slice ham

1 slice processed cheese

1 tablespoon either mustard or mayonnaise

❀ Spread the mustard or mayonnaise over the lettuce leaf. Line with the ham and then the cheese slice. Roll up the lettuce leaf, tucking in any stray edges. Wrap in wax paper and twist the ends to make a secure seal.

Note: These make a great little snack and can be carried to work or to play (for example, the golf course).

Lemon Carrot Muffins

½ cup ground almonds (or walnuts)

¼ cup each, ground sesame and sunflower seeds

½ cup flax meal

¼ cup soy flour

2 packets Splenda

½ teaspoon baking soda

½ teaspoon baking powder

½ teaspoon xanthan gum

¼ teaspoon salt

zest and juice of half a lemon

¼ cup raisins

1 egg, beaten

2 tablespoons olive oil

¼ cup plus 2 tablespoons water

1½ cups finely shredded carrot (2 medium)

Nutrition Information Per Serving	
Calories	169.77
Protein	6.12 g.
Carbs	10.37 g.
Fat	12.29 g.

- ❧ Preheat oven to 375°.
- ❧ The nuts and seeds may be ground in a food processor. The lemon zest needs to be very fine.
- ❧ Mix all dry ingredients together. Mix wet ingredients in a separate bowl.
- ❧ Add wet ingredients to dry and stir to blend. Pour into muffin tins that have been lined with paper muffin cups.
- ❧ Bake for 25 minutes, until brown around the edges.
- ❧ Makes 8 muffins.

Variation: You may use orange juice and zest instead of lemon, but this will increase your carb count slightly. Substitute pumpkin seeds in place of the sesame seeds.

Note: Many thanks again to my sister Stephanie Tompkins for developing this recipe.

Low Carb Citrus Bar

¼ cup soy protein isolate (protein powder)
1 teaspoon cinnamon
1 teaspoon nutmeg
¼ cup pecans (or walnuts)
¼ cup almond slivers
¼ cup sunflower seeds
¼ cup pumpkin seeds
¼ cup unsweetened coconut
4 packets Splenda
3 tablespoons whey protein powder
1 tablespoon xanthan gum
zest of 1 lemon
2 tablespoons olive oil
2 tablespoons no sugar added apricot jam

Nutrition Information Per Serving	
Calories	177
Protein	7.21 g.
Carbs	5.44 g.
Fat	14.94 g.

¼ cup water
2 tablespoons light cream
1 beaten egg

- Preheat oven to 350°. Spray loaf pan with a no stick agent.
- Put all dry ingredients in a food processor and blend well. (I leave a few pieces a bit bigger to provide texture and crunch.)
- Whisk egg and add olive oil, then water and light cream. Finally add jam and fine lemon zest to liquid and blend with whisk.
- Add dry ingredients to the wet and blend with a large spoon. This will make a sticky and heavy batter.
- Place batter in loaf pan and spread evenly with the back of a spoon. Bake for 25 minutes until golden brown at the edges. Let cool and cut into 8 even bars.
- Makes 8 servings.

Variations: Change the flavor with different jams. ED Smith makes a strawberry and a blackberry no sugar added jam that would be nice in these bars.
Note: Thanks to my sister Stephanie Tompkins who did all the difficult preliminary work on these bars.

Low Carb Chocolate Nut Bar

¼ cup soy protein isolate (protein powder)
¼ cup unsalted peanuts
¼ cup pecans (or walnuts)
¼ cup almond slivers
¼ cup sunflower seeds
¼ cup pumpkin seeds
1 tablespoon oat flour
2 tablespoons unsweetened cocoa powder
6 packets Splenda

Nutrition Information Per Serving	
Calories	222.91
Protein	9.56 g.
Carbs	7.32 g.
Fat	18.26 g.

2 tablespoons whey protein powder
2 – 4 tablespoons water
2 tablespoons heavy cream
1 beaten egg
½ tablespoon xanthan gum
1 teaspoon vanilla extract
2 tablespoons olive oil
2 tablespoons peanut butter
2 tablespoons "To Diet For" chocolate flavor protein powder

- ❈ Preheat oven to 350°. Spray loaf pan with a no stick agent.
- ❈ Put all dry ingredients in a food processor and blend well. (I leave a few pieces a bit bigger to provide texture and crunch.)
- ❈ Whisk egg and add olive oil, then water and cream. Finally add peanut butter and vanilla to liquid and blend with whisk.
- ❈ Add dry ingredients to the wet and blend with a large spoon (use just enough water to allow you to blend the mixture). This will make a sticky and heavy batter.
- ❈ Place batter in loaf pan and spread evenly with the back of a spoon. Bake for 25 minutes until golden brown at the edges. Let cool and cut into 8 even bars.
- ❈ Makes 8 servings.

Note: The flavor is somewhat dependent upon the cocoa powder that you use. I use Rapunzel Fully Organic, Unsweetened Cocoa Powder, which is a rich dark chocolate. The cocoa and other ingredients, like the protein isolate and the xanthan gum, are found in health food stores. These freeze well.
Note: Thanks again to my sister Stephanie Tompkins who did all the difficult preliminary work on these bars.

Magic Muffins

2 eggs, separated

5 tablespoons light olive oil

1 teaspoon vanilla

1 teaspoon baking powder

1 teaspoon cinnamon

¼ teaspoon nutmeg

2 packets Splenda

½ cup ground almonds

½ cup ground pecans (or walnuts)

1 cup flax seed meal (or powder)

¼ cup whey (or soy) protein powder

1 cup finely shredded zucchini

1 cup finely shredded cabbage

½ cup finely shredded carrot

½ cup finely chopped cauliflower

Nutrition Information Per Serving	
Calories	193.27
Protein	5.62 g.
Carbs	7.84 g.
Fat	16.60 g.

- Preheat oven to 375°. Line a 12 medium sized muffin tin with paper liners.
- Beat room temperature egg whites with a pinch of salt until stiff peaks form. Set aside.
- Finely shred and chop the vegetables, either by hand or in a food processor. Chop the nuts, or use a food processor on pulse for about 10 seconds. You do not want to pulverize the nuts, but they need to be very small. Combine the nuts and the vegetables and blend well.
- Whisk together the egg yolks, olive oil, vanilla, cinnamon, nutmeg, Splenda and baking powder until well mixed. Add the flax seed meal and the protein powder. This becomes a fairly dense mixture.
- Add the nuts and vegetables to the flax mixture and mix well. Fold in the egg white until blended.

❀ Spoon the mixture into the lined muffin molds. Bake for 30 – 40 minutes until nicely browned on the top.
❀ Makes 12 muffins.

Variations: You can vary the nuts to alter the flavor of these muffins. You may also substitute different vegetables, using yellow summer squash or broccoli, if desired. The flax seed meal needs to be purchased at a health food store. For the protein powder, you can use a vanilla or unflavored protein shake mix if you have one in your cupboard, or purchase one at the health food store. My friend Annette Wall suggested substituting savory seasonings for the cinnamon, to make a savory muffin to have with soup.

Note: Thanks to Valerie Caspersen of Victoria who gave me the idea for these great muffins.

Party Nuts

2 egg whites

1 cup unsalted almonds

1 cup unsalted walnuts

1 cup unsalted pecans

1 cup unsalted peanuts

8 packets Splenda

1 teaspoon cinnamon

1 teaspoon cayenne pepper

½ teaspoon salt

¼ teaspoon nutmeg

Nutrition Information Per Serving	
Calories	157.71
Protein	4.09 g.
Carbs	6.16 g.
Fat	14.12 g.

- ❁ Preheat the oven to 325°. Whisk the egg whites with the salt until foamy. Put the Splenda and the spices in a small bowl and blend together.
- ❁ Put the nuts in a large bowl and pour the foamy egg whites over them and stir to coat. Sprinkle the spices over the nuts and stir well.
- ❁ Spray a cookie sheet with a no-stick agent. Spread the nuts evenly on the cookie sheet and place in the oven for approximately 15-20 minutes, until browned. The nuts need to be stirred frequently to keep from burning.
- ❁ Cool and store in an airtight container.
- ❁ Makes 4 cups.

Note: Nutrition information calculated on a serving size of 1/5 cup.

Salmon Ball

1, 7.5 oz. can of salmon

1, 250 g. package cream cheese

1 tablespoon fresh lemon juice

1 green onion, finely chopped

1½ tablespoons horse-radish

¼ teaspoon paprika

Topping

⅓ cup chopped walnuts

¼ cup fresh chopped parsley

2 tablespoons fresh chopped dill

Nutrition Information Per Serving	
Calories	31.92
Protein	2.28 g.
Carbs	0.36 g.
Fat	2.44 g.

- Cream together first six ingredients with a whisk, until smooth.
- Place the salmon mixture in a small round cereal bowl. Cover with plastic wrap and press the wrap down to the surface of the salmon. Make a tight package. Place in the fridge over night, or at least for 2-3 hours.
- Mix together the ingredients for the topping in a large bowl. Remove the salmon ball from the bowl and roll in the toppings, pressing firmly.
- Place the ball on a serving plate and garnish with fresh dill stems. Serve with sliced cucumber or small low carb crackers.
- Makes approximately 2 cups.

Note: Nutrition information based on 50 servings, and does not include the cracker or cucumber slices.

Note: Thanks to my sisters, Stephanie Tompkins and Kathy Spampinato, each of whom provided ideas for this recipe.

Hearty Vegetable Soup

2 tablespoons light olive oil

2 cloves garlic, minced

1½ tablespoons fresh chopped parsley

1 medium sweet onion, minced

8 cups chicken or beef stock

4 large celery sticks, cut into ½" pieces

1 cup sliced mushrooms

2 cups sliced cabbage

1 cup trimmed green beans

1 cup asparagus spears, cut into 1" pieces

1 medium zucchini, cut into ½" pieces

1 medium carrot, thinly sliced

Nutrition Information Per Serving	
Calories	110.76
Protein	3.07 g.
Carbs	10.99 g.
Fat	7.40 g.

❄ Heat olive oil over medium heat in a large soup pot. Add the onion and garlic and sauté for about 3 – 4 minutes. Add the mushrooms and parsley and continue cooking for 3 or 4 more minutes, until the mushrooms are soft.

❄ Add the chicken (or beef) stock and the cabbage, beans, carrots and cauliflower. Simmer for approximately 1 hour.

❄ Add the asparagus, celery and zucchini and continue to simmer for 15 minutes longer.

❄ Makes 4 servings.

Tip: This soup may be refrigerated and reheated before serving.

French Onion Soup

1 lb. onions (4 cups sliced)

¼ cup butter

3 cloves garlic, minced

6 cups beef bouillon

½ teaspoon salt

fresh ground pepper

1½ cups shredded mozzarella

Nutrition Information Per Serving	
Calories	359.76
Protein	20.58 g.
Carbs	10.58 g.
Fat	26.66 g.

- ❀ Mince the garlic and cut whole, peeled onions into thin rounds.
- ❀ Melt butter in a large soup pot, and add the onion and garlic. Caramelize the onion by cooking it over medium heat until the natural sugar is released and the onion turns brown and is reduced in volume. This will take about 25 to 30 minutes, and the mixture should be stirred frequently.
- ❀ Add the beef bouillon, salt and freshly ground black pepper, reduce the heat and simmer for 35 minutes.
- ❀ To serve, pour the soup into 4 individual oven proof soup bowls. Sprinkle each bowl with shredded cheese, and place all 4 bowls on a cookie sheet.
- ❀ Place the cookie sheet under a hot broiler for 2-3 minutes until the cheese is melted and has browned.
- ❀ Makes 4 servings.

Note: Thanks to my sister Kathy Spampinato who provided the basic recipe for this soup.

Egg Salad

4 hard boiled eggs

1 celery stick, finely minced

1 green onion, finely chopped

¼ cup red or green pepper, finely minced

⅓ cup mayonnaise

1½ teaspoons Dijon mustard

½ teaspoon salt

fresh ground pepper

6 – 8 red lettuce leaves

Nutrition Information Per Serving	
Calories	293.68
Protein	9.61 g.
Carbs	2.79 g.
Fat	28.04 g.

❀ Place 4 eggs in a pot and cover with water. Bring to a boil, reduce heat, and boil for 10 minutes. Rinse the eggs in cold water to cool them, and place in the fridge for at least one hour.

❀ Crack the eggshells and peel off. Roughly chop the eggs. Add the celery, onion and red or green pepper.

❀ Mix the mayonnaise, mustard, salt and pepper. Add the dressing to the egg mixture and mix gently until just blended.

❀ Serve on a bed of red lettuce.

❀ Makes 2 – 3 servings.

Grilled Eggplant

	Nutrition Information
	Per Serving
1 medium eggplant	
1½ - 2 tablespoons light olive oil	Calories 80.96
1 tablespoon fresh chopped parsley	Protein 1.43 g.
1 tablespoon fresh ground pepper	Carbs 8.38 g.
	Fat 5.50 g.

※ Preheat the BBQ or grill to medium heat. Mix the parsley and pepper with the olive oil.

※ Slice the eggplant into slices between ¼ʺ and ½ʺ in thickness. Brush both sides of the eggplant with the olive oil mixture.

※ Place the slices on the grill for 2-3 minutes a side until golden brown grill marks appear and they are cooked through.

※ Makes 4-6 servings, of 2 slices per serving, depending on the size of the eggplant.

Note: Nutrition information calculated based on 4 servings.

Chicken Wrap

4 cabbage leaves

1 cup cooked chicken pieces (cubed or thinly sliced)

½ red onion, thinly sliced

½ red pepper, thinly sliced

½ green pepper, thinly sliced

1 tablespoon olive oil

1 tomato, seeded and finely minced

½ teaspoon salt

½ teaspoon fresh ground pepper

½ cup shredded cheddar cheese

Nutrition Information Per Serving	
Calories	258.0
Protein	28.25 g.
Carbs	12.79 g.
Fat	13.23 g.

- ❁ Rinse the cabbage leaves well, and cut out the hard core. Place with ½" water in a microwave dish and set aside.
- ❁ Mince the tomato, add the salt and pepper, and place in a small serving dish. Grate the cheese and place in small serving dish. Place the chicken pieces in another small dish.
- ❁ Heat the olive oil and sauté the onion and peppers for approximately 7-10 minutes until soft. Just before the vegetables are done, place the cabbage leaves in the microwave and cook for 3-4 minutes on high. Put the vegetables in a small heat proof dish, and bring the cabbage leaves and each of the serving dishes to the table.
- ❁ To serve, take a single cabbage leaf, line it with chicken, onion and peppers, add tomato and sprinkle with grated cheese. Roll up the leaf, tucking in any stray edges.
- ❁ Makes 2 servings, of two wraps each.

Variation: You may substitute cooked beef for the chicken as a variation.

Cabbage Rolls

1 small head of cabbage
1¼ lb. lean ground beef
1 cup finely shredded zucchini
1 celery stick, minced
½ cup finely chopped mushrooms
1 egg
2 tablespoons fresh chopped parsley
½ teaspoon salt
1 teaspoon fresh ground pepper

Nutrition Information Per Serving	
Calories	220.42
Protein	15.49 g.
Carbs	12.19 g.
Fat	12.54 g.

Topping
1 medium onion, minced
½ cup sliced mushrooms
2 tablespoons light olive oil
1 can condensed tomato soup
1 tablespoon fresh chopped parsley

½ cup chopped celery
1 garlic clove, minced
½ cup water

- ❀ Preheat oven to 350°.
- ❀ Remove the core from the cabbage and separate the leaves. Microwave the leaves in ½ cup of water for 5 minutes on high, and set aside.
- ❀ Combine the beef, minced celery, onion and zucchini in a large mixing bowl. Beat the egg slightly and add it to the beef, along with the chopped parsley, salt and pepper. Mix thoroughly.
- ❀ Place approximately ¼ to ⅓ of a cup of the beef mixture in the middle of each cabbage leaf. Roll up, tucking in any edges to make a tight package, and place in a baking dish that has been sprayed with a no stick agent.
- ❀ Sauté garlic, onion, celery and mushrooms in the olive oil over medium heat. Add the tomato soup, water and chopped parsley.
- ❀ Pour the topping over the cabbage rolls, cover and bake for 1 hour and 15 minutes.
- ❀ Makes 10 cabbage rolls.

Chocolate Mint Cake

Cake
½ cup oat flour
½ cup soy flour
⅓ cup unsweetened cocoa powder
½ teaspoon salt
¼ teaspoon baking soda
¼ teaspoon baking powder
¾ cup butter
12 packets Splenda
2 teaspoons vanilla extract
3 large eggs
½ cup light cream
1 cup miniature semisweet chocolate chips

Nutrition Information Per Serving	
Calories	476.26
Protein	8.34 g.
Carbs	32.37g.
Fat	38.21 g.

Filling
1 cup semisweet chocolate chips
½ cup heavy cream
½ teaspoon peppermint extract

Frosting
6 ounces bittersweet chocolate
½ cup heavy cream
½ teaspoon peppermint extract

Garnish
Small red & white mints

Cake
- ❀ Preheat oven to 350°. Butter two 8 inch round cake pans and line with parchment paper. Butter the paper and up the sides of the pan, and dust with oat flour.
- ❀ Bring the butter to room temperature. Whisk together the flour, cocoa powder, salt, baking powder and baking soda until blended.
- ❀ With electric mixer, beat butter until light and fluffy. Add the Splenda, then the vanilla and the eggs, one at a time. Add the dry mixture, alternately with the cream, in two batches each, blending well after each addition. Mix in the chocolate chips.
- ❀ Pour the batter, evenly divided, into the two prepared cake pans. Smooth the batter in the pans until even. Bake in the center of the

oven rack until tester inserted in the middle comes out clean. This will take approximately 40-45 minutes, depending on your oven. Cool on a cake rack for 5 minutes. Turn cake out onto a cooling rack, peel off the parchment, and cool completely.

Filling
- ❧ Place chocolate chips in a medium bowl.
- ❧ Bring cream to a simmer in a small saucepan.
- ❧ Pour the cream over the chocolate chips. Whisk to melt the chocolate and blend. Continue whisking until smooth. Add the peppermint extract and blend.
- ❧ Set aside to cool at room temperature, while cakes cool.
- ❧ When you are ready to assemble (cakes should be completely cool throughout), beat the filling using electric mixer until it is fluffy and light in color. This may take a few minutes. Place the bottom cake on a flat surface and examine the top to make sure it is flat. If necessary, slice a thin piece off the top to even it out. Spread the filling evenly over the top of this cake and place the second cake on top of the filling and gently press down to make sure that it is secure. Chill for 20 minutes before frosting.

Frosting
- ❧ Cut the bittersweet chocolate into small pieces and place in a bowl.
- ❧ Bring the cream to a simmer in a small saucepan.
- ❧ Pour the cream over the chocolate pieces. Whisk to melt the chocolate and blend. Continue whisking until smooth and shiny. Add the peppermint extract and blend. Place the filled cake on a cake rack with wax paper below the rack. Pour the frosting over the cake and let it run down the sides.

Garnish
- ❧ Put a few small red & white mints in the food processor and pulse for a couple of seconds to break them into small pieces. Sprinkle the mint pieces in a boarder around the top of the cake.
- ❧ Makes 10 servings.

> *Note: This delicious cake has a pretty high carb count, so I save it for very special occasions, and have only a small piece.*

Raspberry Cheesecake

Crust

1 cup pecan pieces (or walnut)

1 cup almond pieces

2 packets Splenda

2 tablespoons melted butter

Nutrition Information Per Serving	
Calories	411.90
Protein	11.32 g.
Carbs	9.54 g.
Fat	38.33 g.

Filling

2 packages (250 g. each) of light cream cheese

2 packages (250 g. each) of cream cheese

4 large eggs

¼ cup heavy cream

2 teaspoons vanilla extract

10 packets Splenda

Topping

2 cups fresh (or frozen unsweetened) raspberries

4 packets Splenda

4 teaspoons lemon juice

※ Preheat oven to 325°. Butter a 9¨ spring form pan and set aside.

※ Finely chop the nuts, or put in a food processor and pulse for about 10 seconds. You do not want the nuts to be powdered, but finely chopped. Add the melted butter and the Splenda and mix well. Press the crust into the pan and bake for 10 –12 minutes or until lightly browned. Remove from the oven and let cool.

※ Allow the cream cheese to come to room temperature, and beat with electric mixer until smooth. This is easier to do if you chop the cream cheese into pieces before beating. Add the Splenda and continue beating. Add the eggs one at a time and beat the mixture after each egg. Add the heavy cream and vanilla extract and beat well to mix all ingredients.

❈ Pour the cheese mixture into the spring form pan, and even out the top with a spatula.

❈ Put the raspberries, lemon juice and Splenda into a blender or food processor and puree. (If using frozen berries, they must be completely thawed before blending.) You may strain the puree if you don't like the seeds.

❈ Using approximately ¼ the raspberry puree, drop it by spoonfuls on top of the cheese mixture, distributing the spoonfuls around the perimeter of the pan. Using a sharp knife, 'cut' into the raspberry puree dollops and drag out to points. Do this 2 or 3 times for each dollop of raspberry, making an attractive pattern on top of the cake.

❈ Place the pan in the middle of the oven and bake for 55–60 minutes until set and slightly brown at the edges. Remove from the oven and place on a cookie rack to cool. After about 10 minutes, take a sharp knife and run the blade around the perimeter before loosening the sides of the pan. Let the cheesecake cool completely and then place it in the fridge until serving time. I do not try to take the cake off the bottom of the spring form. If I want to take the cheesecake to the table to serve, I just place the spring form bottom on an attractive serving plate.

❈ To serve, place a piece of cheesecake on a dessert plate and drizzle the plate with the remaining raspberry puree. This is easiest to do with a small squeeze bottle sold in kitchen and dollar stores.

❈ Makes 10 – 12 servings.

CHAPTER 9

Frequently Asked Questions (FAQ's)

*"It is time to take control and responsibility back from those
who are arguing about who has the right answers."*
Harvey and Marilyn Diamond

Patricia has received a number of email messages from readers who have questions concerning low carb eating. Whenever she has had the opportunity to meet readers, at book signings or while doing 'talk show' television, many of the same questions arise. We have answered most of these questions in detail, in the body of our book. We thought you might find it interesting and useful to review the questions from other readers. We present a 'short' version of the answer where we have provided indepth information in the body of the book.

What do you eat for breakfast?

The single most asked question in our experience. Review Chapter 7, Menu Planning, to get the full list of options. You may have eggs any style with bacon, sausage, or ham. Perhaps you might choose cottage cheese or whole plain yogurt with small toppings of fruit or nuts and seeds. Either a low carb shake or a Low Carb Smoothie is a quick and easy option. If you are comfortable with less traditional breakfasts, try a vegetable stir fry or a green salad with nuts or tuna for protein. Almost anything is an option, keeping in mind the carbohydrate content and your daily target.

Does eating low carb mean that I have to give up bread?

During the weight loss period, you should not eat any bread. When you move to maintenance, you give up only the foods you choose. Patricia has not had a piece of bread, or a dinner roll, in over two years. This is her choice, based on our assumption that she is sensitive to wheat. It also makes her food choices very simple and straight forward, because she simply takes bread out of the equation.

Harv still eats bread, although less frequently than before, and only whole grain breads. There are some breads that are marketed as 'low carb' breads, but you need to be aware of the grams of carb per serving and use accordingly. You might also find low carb bread in your grocery store, simply by reading all the labels. We recently found a whole grain bread in the grocery store that has only 12 grams of carb per slice, and Harv found it quite tasty.

Do I have to completely give up potatoes, rice and pasta?

As with bread, these products should not be eaten during the weight loss phase of any low carb approach. Only you can determine how much, if any, of these foods you want to gradually reintroduce into your meal plan as you adapt to a maintenance level. Keep in mind that a medium baked potato with the skin on, has 51 grams of carbohydrate, before you add any garnish! To us, it is not worth it to try to manage the rest of the day with so few carbs just so we can afford to eat a baked potato. This is further reinforced by the fact that potatoes have virtually no nutritional value.

If you feel strongly that you want to reintroduce some of these products into your meal plan, try brown rice (23 grams of carb per ½ cup, cooked) or whole wheat pasta (16 grams of carb per ½ cup cooked spaghetti). Go slowly at first, trying one of these products a week, while you record your intake and monitor your weight. Also pay attention to your body as it deals with these products. If you experience any indigestion, diarrhea, headache or other symptoms, then perhaps you are better off to stay away from these foods.

How much weight can I expect to lose in an average week?

When you start your low carb weight loss plan, you may lose as many as 5 – 7 pounds in the first week. Some of this will be fluid loss as your body adjusts to this approach to food, and as your metabolism 'switches' to fat burning as a mechanism to produce energy. After this initial loss, you will lose anywhere from 1.5 pounds to 3 pounds a week, on average. This average will vary with your weight, your activity level, and your natural metabolism. While Patricia lost an average of 2.5 pounds every week during weight loss, Harv averaged a loss of 4 pounds a week. We recommend that you aim for 1.5 to 2.5 pounds per week.

What foods can cause a stall in weight loss?

There are many foods that can cause a stall in your weight loss, and the determination of which ones affect you will require some trial and error on your part. As we have stated, many people do not tolerate the commercial low carb bars in any quantity, without either stalling or putting on some weight. We would suggest you cut these out first, if you are eating them as a normal part of your daily intake and experience a stall in weight loss.

Other foods that can cause stalls include foods with a high salt content, such as salted nuts, seeds, and pork rinds. Monitor your intake carefully and review the foods that you have been consuming, particularly the snack foods. Some individuals report that foods containing artificial sweeteners can cause stalls.

Lack of exercise can contribute to a stall in weight loss.

How do I get out of a stall?

Once you have done a review of your food diary to determine what might be the cause of your stall, you need to change something. If you can identify the culprit (for example too many low carb bars), then the required change is obvious. If it is not immediately obvious what has caused the stall, you are back to a process of trial and error.

Are you getting enough exercise? If not, try adding a walk at noon everyday – even a 20-minute walk on a daily basis will make a difference. Are you snacking in the evening after dinner? Try some sugar free jello as a snack or sugar free gum to avoid other snacks before bed. What you want to do is to *change* some aspect of your plan to 'kick start' the weight loss again. Sometimes it might mean reducing your daily carb intake to something just a bit lower, to get that metabolism back into high speed. Or maybe you need to add some additional vegetables (the low carb type) and salads to help fill your tummy and add bulk to your meals.

Sometimes you just need to be patient. We have known individuals to stall for as many as 6 or 8 weeks for no apparent reason, and then suddenly start losing again. If you are patient, it will happen. And, even if you are in a stall, you will be maintaining your weight, not gaining, and eating healthy foods, all of which are positive. Do not give up hope. Do not lose faith in the low carb approach. It will work for you if you give it time.

Will the medication I am taking affect the success of my weight loss program?

Most medications act by influencing the body's metabolism in some way. Your low carb eating program also influences metabolism so there are many opportunities for medication to affect the success of a weight loss program. If you are taking any prescribed medication you should seek guidance from your family physician before you start your low carb program. If you want to improve your own understanding of the effect of medication you might want to do some reading on your own. The information provided in the book by Dr. Atkins we have reviewed is easy to understand.

What if I want to splurge and have a pizza one night?

You can make whatever choices you feel are best for you. Harv has indulged in the odd slice of pizza since he began his low carb plan. Remember that pizza has on average about 20 – 25 grams of carb *per slice*! Go ahead and splurge and then you will have to be extra careful and keep your carbohydrate intake very low for the balance of the week. If you splurge on pizza without making any reduction in the balance of your week, be prepared for an increase in your weight at weigh-in time. How much of an increase will depend on how big the splurge was. A caution is that if you indulge in this type of food, you may set yourself up for additional urges over the following few days. There is a way to avoid all of this!

Can I eat Chinese food?

It is relatively easy to go out with friends and have a Chinese dinner, if you are careful about which dishes you chose. We do this every once in a while, just for a change of pace, without negative effects. Patricia doesn't eat any rice on these occasions, although Harv does. We choose lots of vegetable dishes and dishes like cashew chicken and beef with broccoli that are not battered and deep fried. Stay away from the sweet and sour dishes as they will have lots of sugar and the meats will be battered and deep fried. Just think about the type of ingredients that go into the dish and its preparation and you will have a good idea what you want to eat.

What do you do when you go to dinner at a restaurant?

When we go out to eat, we have a routine that works well for us. We usually order either a small green salad or soup to start. We ask our server not to bring a bread basket to our table, so it doesn't tempt us and it doesn't go to waste. We order whatever we have chosen for our main meal, and we ask that any potato or rice be left off our plate. We usually ask for additional vegetables to be substituted for the potato. We have never been refused! If there is some fresh fruit on the menu we might order it for dessert, but more likely we will order herb tea and decaff coffee.

What are the high carb foods I should avoid?

The foods that are high in carbs include breads, baked goods, pasta, potatoes, rice and anything with sugar. High carb vegetables include carrots, peas, corn and beets. All fruits have natural sugars called fructose. The fruits that have high carbohydrate content include bananas, apples, oranges, grapes and raisins.

What are the low carb foods?

Low carb foods include most proteins (eggs, cheeses, fish, poultry, meat and nuts) as well as certain low carb vegetables such as lettuce, celery, cucumber, mushrooms, sprouts, cauliflower, green beans, asparagus, and cabbage.

Are there any medical conditions that would make it unwise to adopt a low carb lifestyle?

There is virtually no medical condition that would prevent you from living a low carb lifestyle. Even so, if you have a medical condition you should consult with your family doctor before you begin your low carb program.

If you have a question that wasn't answered here, we invite you to ask us through our website at www.lowcarbliving.ca.

CHAPTER 10

Low Carb Products and Resources

"The best way to avoid trans fatty acids
is to become a devoted label reader."
Michael R. Eades, M.D. and Mary Dan Eades, M.D.

The popularity of low carb diets and meal plans has resulted in the development of a variety of low carbohydrate products and resources. This is great news for all of us! It provides a wider range of variety and choice in the products we purchase and consume. We have taken the time to test some of these products ourselves, and will share our opinions with you. There are many additional products that we have not had the opportunity to test, and we welcome your feedback and comments on our website, www.lowcarbliving.ca. You will find the majority of the low carb products are found in health food and natural food stores. We are now starting to see these products appear on the shelves of our neighborhood grocery chain, as the low carb market increases.

Low Carb Protein Powders

These protein powders mix with either milk or water to make a 'protein shake'. The shakes may be used as a quick and easy breakfast, a lunch replacement, or a snack at any time during the day. We often mix our two scoops of powder with 2 tablespoons of heavy cream and fill the rest of the container (either a glass or a blender attachment) with water. This mixture makes a really thick, rich and creamy shake, and adds only 1 gram of carb to your count.

You need to pay attention to the protein powder that you purchase to ensure it is a low carb brand. As with all other foods and ingredients when you begin your low carb journey, be sure to read the labels with particular attention to the carb content of a normal sized portion. You will want a protein powder that contains no more than 2-3 grams of carbohydrate per serving. There are a couple of brands that we use on a regular basis.

"To Diet For" protein powder comes in vanilla, strawberry and chocolate flavors. It is now available in our neighborhood grocery store, which makes it convenient to pick up. The bonus with this particular brand is that it will mix quite well without any blender. This makes it a perfect choice for travel when you don't necessarily have access to a blender in the morning. We pack our protein powder in a zip lock bag (easier than the container it comes in) and take a small plastic cup that has a secure lid. We put water and the 2 scoops of powder in the plastic cup, seal with the lid, and shake vigorously. We have instant morning shakes!

Our friend Annette uses a teaspoon of peppermint or almond extract to enhance the flavor of her protein shakes.

"Designer Protein" is another brand that we like. It also comes in vanilla, strawberry and chocolate flavors. This brand does require a blender or immersion blender to get properly mixed, so there are no lumps (ugh!) in the shake.

Trader Joe's (in the United States) have a store brand protein powder that has no carbohydrates at all, according to the label. It is a very inexpensive powder, and has no flavor enhancements. This makes it a slightly unpleasant shake to drink, unless you add a little unsweetened cocoa, some Splenda or a few fresh strawberries to provide some extra flavor. It also needs a blender to get properly mixed in order to go down smoothly.

Dr. Atkins has recently produced a pre-mixed shake that comes in individual containers. We have seen these even in the grocery stores in the U.S., but they have not yet reached Canada. We have not had the opportunity to try these, and cannot comment on their taste. We do note that as with other pre-mixed shakes, the cost of a single serving is considerably higher than with the shakes that you mix yourself. It is all a matter of convenience and personal preference.

There are many additional brands of protein powders and shakes. Make sure that you are trying a low carb option, and experiment until you find the one you like best. We would love to hear from you if you have discovered something new and exciting in the world of protein shakes.

Low Carb Bars

As with the low carb shakes, there are many manufacturers and a huge variety of flavors in the commercial low carb bars. There must be a very large market for these products, as we see new ones popping up on the shelves all the time! Patricia often uses these products as a quick and easy snack between meals, usually eating a ½ bar at a time, and never more than one full bar in a day.

We need to caution readers about using these products on a regular basis. We have heard from some readers that eating these bars causes them to stall in their weight loss. We have friends who have had similar experiences. We weren't sure what the mechanism might be for this re-action, until we ran across a headline on the Internet that may provide an explanation.

ConsumerLab.com, an independent evaluator of nutrition products and dietary supplements in White Plains, New York, announced in October 2001 that "60% of nutrition bars fail to meet claims." They say that of the 30 products they tested, comprised of protein bars, low carb bars and other similar products, only 12 accurately lived up to the claims made on their labels with respect to calories, fat, carbohydrates, sugars, proteins, cholesterol, and sodium. Further, 50%, or 15 of the 30 products they tested, exceeded the levels of carbohydrate on the label by as much as 20 grams. This miscalculation was found in the testing to have oc-curred even among those bars that were labeled 'low carb'.

Apparently, many of the manufacturers of these products do not count the ingredient 'glycerine' in their carbohydrate content. This is so, even though the U.S. Food and Drug Administration (FDA) has ruled that glycerine is a carbohydrate and must be reported as such. We are led to understand that there is some investigation going on at the present time and we might well see a change in the labeling of these products in the near future to more accurately reflect their contents.

In the interim, we are left to wonder about the appropriateness of adding these products to our low carb lifestyle. We became members of the ConsumerLab.com to be able to access the published details of the study. Unfortunately, they provide the names of only the products that accurately reflect the contents on the label, and therefore 'passed' the test. We didn't recognize any of the low carb bars that we occasionally use, in the group listed. The published results do *not* indicate the names of the other products that were tested. So, we do not know if the brands that we are familiar with did not live up to the claims on the label, or simply were not tested as part of this particular sample.

We do caution you to tread lightly with these bars and use them sparingly, particularly at the beginning of your weight loss plan. Some people use them without any undesired side effects, and Patricia is one of these individuals. It appears, however, that they do cause problems for many people. This was a driving force in the development of two home made low carb bars found in Chapter 8, New & Amazing Recipes. These low carb bars have between 7 to 9 grams of carbohydrate in a single serving. It is higher than the commercial products, but you will know every ingredient in the bars, and be able to feel confident about the carb content. The home made low carb bars are also considerably less expensive that the commercial ones. Our comments on the commercial brands follow.

Atkins Advantage Bar

Dr. Atkins has built a huge commercial empire around his low carb diet. One of the main groups of products available are his low carb bars which can be found in grocery stores, and health food stores alike. The Advantage bar claims to have 2.6 grams of carbohydrate per bar, but the label does state that glycerine has not been included in this calculation although it is an ingredient in the bar. These bars come in many flavors and Patricia likes the 'Almond Brownie'.

Ultimate Lo Carb Bar

This product, manufactured by Biochem, is another low carb bar claiming to have only 2 grams of carbohydrate. This label also states that "glycerine is not a carbohydrate", so presumably they have not included it in their calculations, although it is listed as an ingredient. Biochem also produces a large variety of flavors. Patricia used to enjoy the 'Chocolate Nut Brownie', but finds lately that the quality control in the manufacturing process is not very effective. Within the last year, the bars vary dramatically in texture (from smooth and creamy to dry as dust) and flavor (from very rich chocolate to saw dust), depending on the 'batch'. The other complicating factor for us is that this product has become difficult to purchase in Canada. We have not been able to determine why. Even our helpful health food store clerk says that her "Distributor can no longer get them", but she doesn't know why. This problem of supply does not seem to exist in the U.S., and we recently found these bars in a health store in New Zealand!

Protein Revolution

This company produces a wide range of low carb bars. The label claims that only 2.5 grams of carbohydrate are present in each bar. They also claim that glycerine is not a carb, so presumably they mean that they don't include it in their calculation. Some of these bars are extremely close to what we would think of as a regular chocolate bar, in both flavor and texture. They manufacture some sophisticated flavors, and Patricia likes the 'Double Chocolate Fudge Almond'.

Myoplex Low Carb Bar

This new bar is made by a company called EAS out of Golden, Colorado. This company also states that glycerine is included in the calorie count, but not the carbohydrate count. The label states that there are 2.5 grams of carbohydrate in each bar. The flavors include 'Apple Cinnamon' and 'Blueberry'. We thought the Apple Cinnamon was nice and tart, but as with the other bars, we worry about the real carb content.

Designer Whey Protein

This is another relatively new low carb bar on the market. This label states that "this product contains glycerine. Glycerine is not a carbohydrate…" so we presume that it is not included in the carb count of 6 grams of carb. We originally thought it might include glycerine in the carb count, since it is a little higher than other low carb bars. We have tested the 'Creamy Peanut Butter Chocolate' bar, and it is quite tasty. These protein bars are manufactured by Next Proteins in Carlsbad, California.

You may be wondering if Harv ever has any of these bars. The answer is not very often. He does eat, and enjoys, the home made variety that are found in the recipe section. He is not very keen on most of the commercial low carb bars. Harv has many other options for snacks that are not available to Patricia, due to her severe allergy to cheese. In addition, he doesn't feel hunger between meals as Patricia does. So, we each deal with our individual metabolism, needs and preferences. That's how a low carb lifestyle can be flexible and easy for any individual.

Other Low Carb Products

We see more and more low carb products being developed. We have not had occasion to try all of them. Some of these are simply too expensive, in our view, to be worth the cost. We found a 'low carb chocolate chip cookie' in a health food store that cost over $5.00 U.S. for a single cookie! And it wasn't that big! You can find 'low carb' bread and special 'low carb' vitamins these days. If you try any of these we invite you to send your comments to our website, www.lowcarbliving.ca.

Low Carb Ingredients

Your local health food store probably stocks many useful low carb ingredients. We are starting to experiment with some of these ingredients, as you will notice in the recipe section of this book (Chapter 8). (Patricia's cookbook, *Easy Low Carb Cooking*, was designed so that you could make any recipe with the ingredients normally found in your kitchen cupboards.) Some of the ingredients that we are experimenting with include soy flour, soy protein isolate, whey protein powder, oat flour, flax seed and flax seed meal (or powder), xanthan gum (a gluten free thickener) and others. It can be a bit more of a challenge to cook or bake with ingredients that are not familiar at first, but it is also exciting to try whole new ways to approach food preparation. You can find rich, dark unsweetened cocoa in health food stores, with a higher percentage of cocoa than we find in the grocery store.

Other Products

Health food stores and the diabetic aisles in your neighborhood grocery are great places to find new products to try. Get to know the people in your local health food store, and talk to them about your dietary preferences. They can be a wonderful resource for you. Patricia is well known in our local stores, and often has products brought to her attention, that she might otherwise miss.

You can find no sugar added jams and jellies. They are great as a treat sometimes with a meat or poultry dish, or as ingredients in our home made low carb bars. We have found sugar free mints, sugar free fruit flavored candies, and sugar free gum in these locations.

Recently we have allowed ourselves to experiment very cautiously with some sugar free and low carb chocolate and chocolate bars. The brands that we have found include the no sugar added truffles at our local chocolate maker, Purdy's. They produce truffles that taste delicious and contain 4 grams of carb each. Of course, you can't have many at this level, and if you are someone who can't stop if you have one, you will want to stay away from products like these. We are able to eat one or two, every once in a while and not need any more. It is especially nice to have this option around the holidays, when everyone seems to be eating chocolate.

Our local health food store carries chocolate bars made by Ross Chocolates. These bars, which come in many flavors (such as Raspberry Delight, Crunchy Delight and White Chocolate), have no sugar added and contain 2.7 grams of carbohydrate per bar. This information is not available on the label, unfortunately, but if you ask your friendly clerk, they should be able to provide you with a sheet of information about the contents. We presume these were originally developed for diabetics, who used to be more concerned with sugar than carbs, although this too is changing.

We have a caution related to both of these products, and many other low carb chocolates. For the majority of these products you will note when you read the label that they contain Maltitol as a sweetner. Maltitol is a member of a group of sweeteners known as sugar alcohols. They are very sweet, significantly lower in calories than sugar, and non-carcinogenic. Maltitol has been approved as a 'safe' ingredient and alternative to sugar. It is found in many sugar free hard candies, chewing gums, chocolates, baked goods and ice cream. Most labels warn that Maltitol can have a laxative effect when consumed in high levels and therefore, you need to be cautious as a consumer. We have tried both the above products and others, that contain sugar alcohols, without any laxative affects. We do not overindulge in these products, often sharing a single chocolate bar between us. We do not splurge on this type of food very often, probably averaging not more than one a month. As with so many other things, it is better to err on the side of caution.

Carbolite is another sugar free chocolate bar. It is made with Splenda, and the label reports that it has 0 grams of carbohydrate. This product also contains Maltitol, in addition to the Splenda. These bars are found in the U.S. and can be purchased at most Seven Eleven stores. The flavors include 'Chocolate Peanut Butter' and 'Chocolate Almond'.

We are aware of another low carb chocolate bar called 'Pure DeLite' whose manufacturer also makes a low carb chocolate truffle. This product is available in the U.S. in health food stores.

There is a Swiss company, Chocolat Stella Premium, which manufactures a wide variety of no sugar added chocolate bars. These are somewhat higher in carbs (approximately 13 grams per serving) than the products made especially for diabetics or dieters, but still within reasonable limits, if eaten only occasionally. We bought some in New Zealand where the other brands of low carb chocolates are not as readily available.

Look in the freezer section of your grocery store for 'lite' ice creams, many of which are 'no sugar added' varieties. Breyers Light vanilla ice cream has approximately 15 grams of carbohydrate in a ½ cup serving. Add just a few sliced strawberries and you have a real treat. These are the sorts of things that we do occasionally now that we are on maintenance, that make this approach to eating so flexible. You can have dessert that contains 20 grams of carbohydrate, as long as the rest of your intake is moderate. You won't want to make this a habit though, even on maintenance.

The Dairy Queen has a couple of low sugar frozen products they manufacture primarily for diabetics. We have tried these and they taste great, but are a little higher in carbs than other products, averaging about 17 grams per serving. These Dairy Queen products contain both sorbitol, which is another sugar alcohol, and aspartame. We caution you to tread lightly when experimenting with these products.

We need to reiterate that we indulge in these treats *infrequently*. We did not even try any of this type of low carb product during the first year we were on our low carb plan. We think it is best to go slowly and cautiously in this regard. If you are an individual who has difficulty controlling your food intake, or if you are one of the many individuals who has food cravings and urges, these products might not be for you. We have heard that for some people, eating any of these types of products can bring back sugar cravings and/or make them feel unwell. For all these reasons, please go slowly when experimenting with chocolates or other treats.

Low Carb Resources

As we mentioned in the early chapters of our book, there are so many low carb resources available in the market today it has become confusing and perhaps frustrating to sort through them. We recently stopped in a large bookstore and were able to count over 35 books in the low carb section alone! We hope that we have helped you understand some of the most popular of these, so you can decide whether one or another is most appropriate for you. Or, perhaps you will choose to try a general low carb approach, as described in this book. To review the diet books that we have examined, please refer to Chapter 3.

The Internet is increasingly a good source of information and support for 'low carbers'. If you log onto a website, please be aware that each site may have a particular emphasis regarding the information they provide. For example, Dr. Atkins' sites (there are a few) will have his diet, his advice and his products as the main sources of information. There are some generic sites that provide a wide range of services, including forums (like chat rooms, but not live) as well as product and research information. These sites, and their web addresses, can change quickly. We would, however, like to provide a couple of addresses for you to get started.

Lowcarb.ca is a Canadian based low carb site that is administered out of Vancouver, B.C. It is one of the best administered and easiest to navigate of the sites we have found. Patricia is a registered user of this site, and occasionally goes in and participates in the forums. There is no charge to join, and the discussions can be quite interesting and enlightening. This site has product and research information, in addition to member forums and polls. The level of activity is astonishing, with many thousands of 'hits' every month. There are a couple of things that Patricia particularly likes about this site. The webmaster or administrator sends out monthly reviews to all registered users, to keep you up to date on the activity of the site and highlight some of the more active topics. The webmaster will notify you directly, through your email address, if a topic (they are called threads) that you have participated in has had any information added. It is a well designed and 'user friendly' site. The participants come from all over North America as well as England, New Zealand and Australia . It is a very supportive environment, and almost without exception, the interactions and discussions are helpful. Please remember these are ordinary people like you and I who are sharing their personal experiences in dealing with low carb concerns, they are not professionals.

Another generic site based out of the U.S. is a huge site called **Delphi.com**. This site is not dedicated entirely to low carb topics like the previous one, but it has a number of low carb forums and discussion groups if you do a search. Patricia has navigated around this site and finds that it does provide some information, but in her opinion, it is not as well managed or as well monitored as Lowcarb.ca.

There is a website called **Fitday.com** where you can record your daily food intake, should you wish to do this on line, rather than in hard copy as we do. There is an Atkins fan club on the Internet at **Atkinsfanclub.com** and the general Atkins site is located at **Atkinscenter.com**. Another general site is located at **CarbSmart.com** based in California. We cannot comment on its administration, as we have not spent any time at this site. **Netrition.com** is a general nutrition site that is not low carb specific, but has great information on nutrition and current research, if you are inclined. Almost without exception, the books that we have reviewed each has a website.

Our website at www.lowcarbliving.ca provides a number of interesting features. You will find:

- Recipes: exciting new recipes from Patricia as well as a section for participants to exchange recipe ideas
- Food Diary: a computer version of our food diary that you can download and print for easy use
- Newsletter: this section will keep you up to date on new ideas and any important emerging research
- Photo Album: we have included photographs, both before and after our low carb program. This album also includes many photos of the recipes found in the cookbook, *Easy Low Carb Cooking*, and Chapter 8, New & Amazing Recipes
- What People Are Saying: what other readers and the media are saying about this book and *Easy Low Carb Cooking*
- North American Book Tour: highlights, including photographs, of interesting and humorous experiences during our North American Book Tour
- Frequently Asked Questions: immediately available answers to those questions we get asked most often
- Contact us: allows you to get in touch with us if you have questions or comments about our books or your experience with low carb living

37½   33   31   19½   135

CHAPTER 11

Your Personal Food Diary

"You cannot gain power over food if you don't know what you're eating."
Elson M. Haas, M.D.

Food Diary

Day 1 _____ **Carbs**

Breakfast _____ _____

_____ _____

Lunch _____ _____

_____ _____

_____ _____

_____ _____

Dinner _____ _____

_____ _____

_____ _____

_____ _____

Snacks _____ _____

_____ _____

_____ _____

_____ _____

Daily Total

Excercise/Notes

_____

_____

_____

_____

Food Diary

Day 2 _____ **Carbs**

Breakfast _____ _____
_____ _____
_____ _____
_____ _____

Lunch _____ _____
_____ _____
_____ _____
_____ _____

Dinner _____ _____
_____ _____
_____ _____
_____ _____

Snacks _____ _____
_____ _____
_____ _____
_____ _____
_____ _____

Daily Total ▢

Excercise/Notes

_____
_____
_____
_____
_____
_____
_____

Food Diary

Day 3 _____ **Carbs**

Breakfast _____ _____
_____ _____
_____ _____
_____ _____
Lunch _____ _____
_____ _____
_____ _____
_____ _____
_____ _____
Dinner _____ _____
_____ _____
_____ _____
_____ _____
_____ _____
Snacks _____ _____
_____ _____
_____ _____
_____ _____
_____ _____

Daily Total

Excercise/Notes

_____
_____
_____
_____
_____
_____
_____

Food Diary

Day 4 _____ **Carbs**

Breakfast _____ _____
_____ _____
_____ _____

Lunch _____ _____
_____ _____
_____ _____
_____ _____
_____ _____

Dinner _____ _____
_____ _____
_____ _____
_____ _____
_____ _____

Snacks _____ _____
_____ _____
_____ _____
_____ _____
_____ _____

Daily Total

Excercise/Notes

_____
_____
_____
_____
_____
_____

Food Diary

Day 5 _____ **Carbs**

Breakfast _____ _____
          _____ _____
          _____ _____
          _____ _____

Lunch   _____ _____
          _____ _____
          _____ _____
          _____ _____

Dinner   _____ _____
          _____ _____
          _____ _____
          _____ _____

Snacks   _____ _____
          _____ _____
          _____ _____
          _____ _____
          _____ _____

Daily Total   [   ]

Excercise/Notes

_____
_____
_____
_____
_____
_____
_____

Food Diary

Day 6 _____ **Carbs**

Breakfast _____ _____

_____ _____

_____ _____

Lunch _____ _____

_____ _____

_____ _____

_____ _____

_____ _____

Dinner _____ _____

_____ _____

_____ _____

_____ _____

_____ _____

Snacks _____ _____

_____ _____

_____ _____

_____ _____

_____ _____

Daily Total [____]

Excercise/Notes

_____

_____

_____

_____

_____

_____

_____

Food Diary

Day 7 _____ **Carbs**

Breakfast _____ _____
           _____ _____
           _____ _____
           _____ _____
Lunch   _____ _____
           _____ _____
           _____ _____
           _____ _____
Dinner   _____ _____
           _____ _____
           _____ _____
           _____ _____
Snacks   _____ _____
           _____ _____
           _____ _____
           _____ _____
           _____ _____

Daily Total   [   ]

Excercise/Notes

_____
_____
_____
_____
_____
_____
_____

Food Diary

Weekly Summary

Weight [   ]

	Total Carbs		Exercise
Day 1	_____		_____
Day 2	_____		_____
Day 3	_____		_____
Day 4	_____		_____
Day 5	_____		_____
Day 6	_____		_____
Day 7	_____		_____
Total	_____		_____
divide by 7	_____		_____
Average	[ ]		[ ]

Notes

_____
_____
_____
_____
_____
_____
_____

Food Diary

Day 1 _____ **Carbs**

Breakfast _____ _____
         _____ _____
         _____ _____
         _____ _____

Lunch   _____ _____
         _____ _____
         _____ _____
         _____ _____

Dinner   _____ _____
         _____ _____
         _____ _____
         _____ _____

Snacks   _____ _____
         _____ _____
         _____ _____
         _____ _____

Daily Total

Excercise/Notes

_____
_____
_____
_____
_____
_____

Food Diary

Day 2 _____ **Carbs**

Breakfast _____ _____
_____ _____
_____ _____
_____ _____

Lunch _____ _____
_____ _____
_____ _____
_____ _____

Dinner _____ _____
_____ _____
_____ _____
_____ _____

Snacks _____ _____
_____ _____
_____ _____
_____ _____

Daily Total

Excercise/Notes

_____
_____
_____
_____
_____
_____
_____

Food Diary

Day 3 _____ **Carbs**

Breakfast _____ _____
           _____ _____
           _____ _____
           _____ _____
Lunch   _____ _____
           _____ _____
           _____ _____
           _____ _____
           _____ _____
Dinner   _____ _____
           _____ _____
           _____ _____
           _____ _____
           _____ _____
Snacks   _____ _____
           _____ _____
           _____ _____
           _____ _____
           _____ _____

Daily Total

Excercise/Notes

_____
_____
_____
_____
_____
_____
_____

Food Diary

Day 4 _____ **Carbs**

Breakfast _____ ____

_____ ____

_____ ____

_____ ____

Lunch _____ ____

_____ ____

_____ ____

_____ ____

_____ ____

Dinner _____ ____

_____ ____

_____ ____

_____ ____

Snacks _____ ____

_____ ____

_____ ____

_____ ____

_____ ____

Daily Total [ ]

Excercise/Notes

_____

_____

_____

_____

_____

_____

_____

Food Diary

Day5 _____ **Carbs**

Breakfast _____ _____
_____ _____
_____ _____

Lunch _____ _____
_____ _____
_____ _____
_____ _____

Dinner _____ _____
_____ _____
_____ _____
_____ _____

Snacks _____ _____
_____ _____
_____ _____
_____ _____
_____ _____

Daily Total

Excercise/Notes

_____
_____
_____
_____
_____
_____
_____

Food Diary

Day 6 _____ **Carbs**

Breakfast _____ ____
_____ ____
_____ ____
_____ ____

Lunch _____ ____
_____ ____
_____ ____
_____ ____

Dinner _____ ____
_____ ____
_____ ____
_____ ____

Snacks _____ ____
_____ ____
_____ ____
_____ ____
_____ ____

Daily Total

Excercise/Notes

_____
_____
_____
_____
_____
_____

Food Diary

Day 7 _____ **Carbs**

Breakfast _____ _____
_____ _____
_____ _____

Lunch _____ _____
_____ _____
_____ _____
_____ _____

Dinner _____ _____
_____ _____
_____ _____
_____ _____

Snacks _____ _____
_____ _____
_____ _____
_____ _____

Daily Total ⬚

Excercise/Notes

_____
_____
_____
_____
_____
_____
_____

Food Diary

Weekly Summary

Weight [ ]

	Total Carbs		**Exercise**
Day 1	_____		_____
Day 2	_____		_____
Day 3	_____		_____
Day 4	_____		_____
Day 5	_____		_____
Day 6	_____		_____
Day 7	_____		_____
Total	_____		_____
divide by 7	_____		_____
Average	[ ]		[ ]

Notes

_____

_____

_____

_____

_____

_____

_____

Chapter 12

Easy Carbohydrate Counter

"When we eat too much carbohydrate, we're essentially send-ing a hormonal message, via insulin, to the body... 'Store fat'."
Barry Sears, Ph.D.

Food	Serving size	Carb gm
Acorn Squash, baked, cubed	½ cup	14.9
Acorn Squash, boiled, mashed	½ cup	10.7
Alfalfa Seeds, Sprouted, Raw	1 cup	1.3
Allspice, Ground	1 tbsp	4.3
Almond Butter	1 tbsp	3.4
Almonds, Dried	22 kernels	5.8
Almonds, Dry Roasted	1 oz	6.9
Almonds, Honey Roasted	1 oz	7.9
Almonds, Oil Roasted	1 oz	4.5
Anchovy, fresh or canned in oil		0.0
Anise Seed	1 tbsp	3.5
Apple, fresh with peel	2¾"	21.1
Apple, fresh with peel, sliced	½ cup	8.4
Apple, fresh, peeled	2¾"	19.0
Apple, fresh, peeled, sliced	½ cup	8.2
Apple, dried, sulfured, uncooked	2 oz	37.4
Apple Butter	1 tbsp	8.6
Apple Juice	8 fl oz	28.8
Applesauce, Sweetened	½ cup	25.5
Applesauce, Unsweetened	½ cup	13.8
Apricot, fresh	3 medium	11.8

Food	Serving size	Carb gm
Apricot, fresh, pitted, halves	½ cup	8.6
Apricots, canned, in juice	½ cup	15.3
Apricots, canned, heavy syrup, with skin	½ cup	27.6
Apricots, dried, sulfured	2 oz	35.0
Apricot nectar	6 fl oz	27.1
Arrowroot, boiled	1" corm	1.9
Artichoke, globe, fresh, boiled	1 medium	15.1
Artichoke hearts, fresh, boiled	½ cup	9.4
Arugula, raw, trimmed	½ cup	4.1
Asparagus, fresh, boiled	4 spears	2.5
Asparagus, frozen, boiled	4 spears	2.9
Asparagus, canned with liquid	½ cup	2.8
Avocados, California, raw	1 medium	12.0
Avocados, California, pureed	½ cup	8.0
Bacon, cooked	2 slices	0
Bacon Bits, real	1 tbsp	0
Bacon Bits, imitation	1½ tbsp	2.0
Bagel, plain	3½" dia	37.9
Bagel, egg	3½" dia	37.6
Baked Beans, plain	½ cup	26.1
Baked Beans with franks	½ cup	19.7
Baked Beans with pork, in sweet sauce	½ cup	26.5
Baked Beans with pork, in tomato sauce	½ cup	24.4
Baking Powder and Baking Soda	1 tsp	0
Bamboo Shoots, fresh, raw, ½" slices	½ cup	4.0
Bamboo Shoots, fresh, boiled, ½" slices	½ cup	1.2
Bamboo Shoots, canned	½ cup	2.1
Banana, raw	8¾" long	26.7
Banana Chips	1 oz	16.6
Barbecue Sauce	2 tbsp	10.0
Barley, pearled, cooked	1 cup	44.3
Basil, fresh	6 med lvs	0.2
Basil, dried, crumbled	1 tsp	0.9
Bass, no added ingredients		0.0
Bay Leaf, dried, crumbled	1 tbsp	0.9
Bean Sprouts, fresh	1 oz	1.9

Food	Serving size	Carb gm
Bean Sprouts, canned	1 cup	1.0
Beechnuts, dried	1 oz	9.5
Beef, any cut		0.0
Beef, Corned		0.5
Beef, gravy	¼ cup	4.0
Beef, jerky, chopped	1 oz	4.1
Beer, regular	12 fluid oz	13.2
Beer, light	12 fluid oz	4.8
Beet, fresh, boiled	½ cup	10.0
Beet, canned	½ cup	6.1
Beet, canned, pickled	½ cup	18.5
Beet Greens, raw	½ cup	0.8
Beet Greens, boiled	½ cup	1.9
Biscuit, plain or buttermilk	1.2 oz pce	17.0
Biscuit, dry mix	2 oz piece	27.6
Biscuit, refrigerated dough, baked	1 oz piece	13.5
Black Bean, dried, boiled	½ cup	20.4
Black Bean Sauce	1 tbsp	2.0
Blackberries, fresh	1 cup	18.7
Bloody Mary, prepared from recipe	8 fl oz	7.2
Blueberries, canned in heavy syrup	½ cup	28.2
Blueberries, fresh	½ cup	10.2
Blueberries, dried	¼ cup	33.2
Bluefish, no added ingredients		0.0
Bologna, Beef or Pork	1 med slice	0.3
Bouillon, beef flavor, dehydrated	1 cube	0.6
Bouillon, chicken flavor, dehydrated	1 cube	1.1
Bourbon & Soda, prepared from recipe	1 fl oz	0.0
Boysenberry, fresh	1 cup	18.7
Bran, see "Cereals" and specific grains		
Bratwurst, pork, cooked	1 oz	1.0
Brazil Nuts, shelled	8 kernels	4.3
Bread, French	1 slice	14.7
Bread, Italian	1 slice	15.0
Bread, mixed grain	1 slice	13.1
Bread, oat bran	1 slice	12.0

Food	Serving size	Carb gm
Bread, oatmeal	1 slice	13.8
Bread, pita, white	6½" dia	33.4
Bread, protein	1 slice	12.4
Bread, pumpernickel	1 slice	15.0
Bread, raisin	1 slice	14.8
Bread, rice bran	1 slice	12.3
Bread, rye	1 slice	16.0
Bread, wheat	1 slice	13.4
Bread, wheat bran or wheat germ	1 slice	17.0
Bread, white	1 slice	14.0
Bread, whole wheat	1 slice	13.1
Bread crumbs, dry, grated	¼ cup	19.5
Breadstick	4 oz stick	6.8
Broad Beans, fresh, raw	½ cup	6.4
Broad Beans, fresh, boiled	4 oz	11.5
Broad Beans, mature, dried, boiled	½ cup	16.7
Broad Beans, mature, canned with liquid	½ cup	15.9
Broccoli, raw, chopped	½ cup	2.0
Broccoli, fresh, boiled, 1 stalk	6.3 oz	3.9
Brown Gravy, mix, prepared	¼ cup	3.3
Brownie	2 oz piece	35.8
Brussel Sprouts, fresh, boiled	½ cup	6.9
Butter, any kind		0.0
Buttermilk, see "Milk"		
Butternut squash, fresh, baked, cubed	½ cup	10.7
Butternut squash, frozen, boiled, mashed	½ cup	12.1
Butterscotch topping	2 tbsp	27.0
Cabbage, raw, shredded	½ cup	1.9
Cabbage, boiled, shredded	½ cup	3.4
Cabbage, Chinese, raw	1 cup	1.4
Cabbage, Chinese, boiled	1 cup	3.2
Cabbage, Red, raw, shredded	1 cup	4.6
Cabbage, Red, boiled, shredded	1 cup	7.2
Cake, angel food, 12 oz cake	1/12	16.4
Cake, Boston Cream, 20 oz cake	1/12	19.8
Cake, cheesecake	1 oz piece	7.2

Food	Serving size	Carb gm
Cake, chocolate, 18 oz cake	1/12	23.8
Cake, coffee cheese	1 oz piece	12.8
Cake, fruitcake	1 oz piece	17.8
Cake, pound	1 oz piece	14.9
Cake, sponge, 16 oz cake	1/12	23.2
Cake mix, angel food, 9" cake	1/12	29.3
Cake mix, carrot, with icing, 9" cake	1/12	32.7
Cake mix, cheesecake, 9" cake	1/12	23.9
Cake mix, chocolate devil's, 9" cake	1/12	31.8
Cake mix, Black Forest, icing, 9" cake	1/12	55.1
Cake mix, gingerbread, 9" cake	1/12	26.3
Cake mix, white without icing, 9" cake	1/12	34.4
Candy, After Eight	5 pieces	32.0
Candy, Baby Ruth	2.1 oz bar	37.2
Candy, Life Savers, butter rum	4 pieces	20.0
Candy, Butterfinger	2.1 oz bar	41.0
Candy, Caramels	1 oz	21.8
Candy, Caramels, chocolate covered	1 oz	24.7
Candy, Chocolate, Milk	1 oz	16.8
Candy, gum, chewing	1 piece	2.9
Candy, gumdrops	1 oz	28.0
Candy, hard candy	1 oz	19.3
Candy, jellybeans	10 large	26.4
Candy, Kit Kat	1.5 oz bar	25.8
Candy, M & M's Plain	1 oz	19.3
Candy, Mars	1.76 oz bar	31.4
Candy, Marshmallows	1 oz	23.0
Candy, Milky Way	2.15 oz bar	43.7
Candy, Mr. Goodbar	2.8 oz bar	40.5
Candy, Oh! Henry	2 oz bar	36.9
Candy, Peanut Brittle	1 oz	19.7
Candy, Peanuts, milk chocolate coated	1 oz	14.0
Candy, Raisins, milk chocolate coated	1 oz	19.4
Candy, Reese's Pieces	1.96 oz pkg	34.1
Candy, Skittles	2.3 oz pkg	62.4
Candy, Skor	1.4 oz bar	22.1

Food	Serving size	Carb gm
Candy, Snickers	2.16 oz bar	36.8
Candy, 3 Musketeers	2.13 oz bar	46.1
Candy, Twizzlers	2.5 oz pkg	65.9
Cane Syrup	1 tbsp	13.4
Cantaloupe	½ x 5" dia	22.3
Caraway Seed	1 tbsp	3.5
Cardamom, Ground	1 tbsp	4.1
Carrots, Whole, fresh, raw	7½" long	7.3
Carrots, Baby, fresh, raw	1 large	1.2
Carrots, fresh, raw, shredded	½ cup	5.6
Carrots, fresh, boiled, sliced	½ cup	8.2
Carrots, frozen, boiled, sliced	½ cup	5.8
Cashew Nuts, dry roasted	14 large	9.3
Cashew Nuts, oil roasted	14 large	8.1
Catsup	1 tbsp	4.1
Cauliflower, boiled	½ cup	2.5
Cauliflower, raw	½ cup	5.0
Cauliflower, Green, boiled	½ cup	3.7
Cauliflower, Green, raw	½ cup	3.0
Celeriac, boiled	½ cup	4.6
Celeriac, raw	½ cup	10.4
Celery, raw	7½" stock	1.5
Celery, boiled, diced	1 cup	6.0
Celery Seed	1 tbsp	2.5
Celery Salt	1 tsp	0.6
Cereal, hot, oatmeal	½ cup	22.5
Cereal, cold, bran flakes	1 cup	22.0
Cereal cold, bran flakes with raisins	1 cup	43.0
Cereal, cold, corn flakes	1 cup	26.0
Cereal, cold, granola	½ cup	40.0
Cereal, cold, multigrain	1 cup	25.0
Cereal, cold, oat bran	1 cup	30.0
Cereal, cold, oats	1 cup	24.0
Cereal, cold, rice	1 cup	35.0
Cereal, cold, piffed rice	1 cup	15.0
Cereal, cold, shredded wheat	2 pieces	38.0

Food	Serving size	Carb gm
Chard, Swiss, boiled, chopped	1 cup	7.0
Chard, Swiss, raw	1 cup	1.4
Cheese, Blue	1 oz	0.6
Cheese, Brick	1 oz	0.8
Cheese, Brie or Camembert	1 oz	0.1
Cheese, Cheddar	1 oz	0.4
Cheese, Colby	1 oz	0.7
Cheese, Cottage, 1% Fat	1 oz	0.8
Cheese, Cottage, 2% Fat	1 oz	1.0
Cheese, Cream	1 oz	0.8
Cheese, Edam	1 oz	0.3
Cheese, Goat, soft type	1 oz	0.3
Cheese, Gouda	1 oz	0.6
Cheese, Limburger	1 oz	0.1
Cheese, Monterey	1 oz	0.2
Cheese, Mozzarella, part skim milk	1 oz	0.8
Cheese, Mozzarella, whole milk	1 oz	0.6
Cheese, Muenster	1 oz	0.3
Cheese, Parmesan, grated	1 tbsp	0.2
Cheese, Parmesan, hard	1 oz	0.8
Cheese, Parmesan, shredded	1 tbsp	0.2
Cheese, Ricotta, part skim milk	1 oz	1.5
Cheese, Ricotta, whole milk	1 oz	0.9
Cheese, Romano	1 oz	1.1
Cheese, Roquefort	1 oz	0.6
Cheese, Sauce	2 tbsp	2.0
Cheese, Sauce Mix, prepared	½ cup	7.0
Cheese Spread, processed, American,	1 oz	2.5
Cheese, Swiss	1 oz	1.0
Cherries, fresh, sour, red, with pitts	½ cup	6.3
Cherries, fresh, sour, red, without pitts	½ cup	9.4
Cherries, fresh, sweet, red, with pitts	½ cup	12.0
Cherries, sour, red, canned, light syrup	½ cup	24.3
Cherries, sour, red, canned, heavy syrup	½ cup	29.8
Cherry Juice	8 fl oz	30.0
Chervil, dried	1 tbsp	1.0

Food	Serving size	Carb gm
Chestnuts, Chinese, raw	1 oz	9.6
Chestnuts, Chinese, dried	1 oz	22.7
Chestnuts, European, roasted	1 cup	75.8
Chestnuts, Japanese, dried	1 oz	23.1
Chestnuts, Japanese, raw	1 oz	9.8
Chestnuts, Japanese, roasted	1 oz	12.6
Chicken, no added ingredients		0.0
Chicken gravy, canned	¼ cup	3.0
Chicken, lunch meat	1 oz	1.0
Chickpeas, dry, boiled	½ cup	22.5
Chicory Greens, raw, chopped	1 cup	9.0
Chicory Roots, raw	1 root	10.8
Chili, canned with beans	I cup	30.0
Chili Powder	1 tbsp	4.4
Chives, fresh or freeze dried, chopped	1 tbsp	0.1
Chocolate, baking, bar, unsweetened	1 oz	8.0
Chocolate chips	½ oz	10.0
Chocolate milk	1 cup	25.9
Chocolate syrup	2 tbsp	24.8
Chocolate flavor beverage mix, powder	3 lg tsp	19.8
Cilantro, raw	¼ cup	0.4
Cinnamon, ground	1 tbsp	5.6
Citrus fruit juice drink	8 fl oz	28.4
Clam, boiled or steamed	9 large	5.8
Clam Chowder, see "Soup"		
Cloves, Ground	1 tsp.	1.4
Club Soda	10 fl oz	0.0
Cocoa, baking, unsweetened	1 tbsp	3.0
Cocoa Mix, Nestle, Hot Cocoa Mix	1 envelope	24.4
Coconut Meat, fresh, shredded	1 cup	12.0
Coconut, canned, flaked, sweetened	⅓ cup	10.5
Coconut Milk, canned	1 tbsp	0.4
Cod, no added ingredients		0.0
Coffee, brewed	6 fl oz	0.8
Coffee, instant, regular, powder	1 tsp	0.4
Coffee, instant, w/sugar, cappuccino flavor	2 tsp round	10.5

Food	Serving size	Carb gm
Coleslaw	½ cup	4.0
Collards, fresh, raw	½ cup	1.2
Collards, fresh, boiled	½ cup	4.1
Collards, frozen, chopped	½ cup	6.1
Cookie, animal crackers	1 oz	21.0
Cookie, chocolate chip	1 oz	18.9
Cookie, chocolate sandwich, cream filled	1 oz	19.9
Cookie, chocolate wafers	1 oz	20.5
Cookie, Fig Newtons, 2 pieces	1 oz	20.0
Cookie, fortune	1 oz	23.8
Cookie, fudge	1 oz	22.2
Cookie, gingersnaps	1 oz	21.8
Cookie, graham crackers	1 oz	21.8
Cookie, marshmallow chocolate	1 oz	17.0
Cookie, oatmeal, fat free	1 oz	22.2
Cookie, peanut butter	1 oz	16.7
Cookie, raisin, soft	1 oz	19.3
Cookie, shortbread	1 oz	19.0
Cookie, sugar	1 oz	19.2
Cookie, vanilla sandwich, cream filled	1 oz	20.4
Coriander, fresh	¼ cup	0.1
Coriander, dried, leaf	1 tsp	0.3
Coriander, dried, seed	1 tsp	0.9
Corn, fresh, boiled, kernel	½ cup	20.6
Corn, canned, kernel	½ cup	15.2
Corn, canned, cream style	½ cup	23.2
Corn, frozen, kernel	½ cup	18.3
Corn, on the cob, boiled	8 oz ear	29.4
Corn Chips, cheese curls	1 oz	16.0
Corn Chips, tortilla chips	1 oz	19.0
Corn Flour (or Cornmeal), whole grain	¼ cup	22.5
Corn Grits, cooked	½ cup	15.7
Corn Relish	1 tbsp	5.0
Corn Syrup	2 tbsp	30.0
Cornstarch	1 tbsp	7.0
Corned Beef Loaf, jellied	1 slice	0.0

Food	Serving size	Carb gm
Crab, Alaska King, imitation, surimi	3 oz	8.5
Crab, Alaska King, no added ingredients		0.0
Crab, Blue, no added ingredients		0.0
Crab, Dungeness, boiled or steamed	3 oz	0.8
Crab, canned		0.0
Crabapples, fresh, with peels	½ cup	11.0
Cracker, cheese	½ oz	8.3
Cracker, crispbread, rye	½ oz	11.6
Cracker, melba toast	½ oz	10.9
Cracker, rye wafers	½ oz	11.4
Cracker, saltines	½ oz	10.2
Cracker, slatines, fat free	½ oz	12.0
Cracker, snack type	½ oz	8.7
Cracker, wheat	½ oz	9.2
Cranberry, fresh, chopped	½ cup	7.1
Cranberry Juice Cocktail	8 fl oz	35.4
Cranberry Sauce, canned, sweetened	½ cup	54.0
Crayfish, no added ingredients		0.0
Cream, Half And Half	1 tbsp	0.6
Cream, whipping, unwhipped	1 tbsp	0.4
Cream, sour, regular	2 tbsp	1.0
Cream, sour, non fat	2 tbsp	4.0
Cream Substitute, powdered	1 tsp	4.1
Creamer, nondairy	1 tsp	1.1
Creme De Menthe, 72 Proof	1 fl oz	14.3
Cream Soda	8 fl oz	32.0
Croissant, plain, buttered	2 oz piece	26.1
Croutons, plain	½ cup	11.0
Cucumber, peeled, raw	8¼" long	8.3
Cucumber, sliced	½ cup	1.6
Cumin Seed, ground	1 tsp	0.9
Currants, European Black, raw	½ cup	8.4
Currants, red or white, raw	½ cup	7.8
Currants, Zante, dried	½ cup	53.3
Curry Powder	1 tsp	1.2
Custard, mix, with milk and egg	½ cup	23.4

Food	Serving size	Carb gm
Dandelion Greens, raw, chopped	1 cup	5.0
Danish Pastry, cheese	2.5 oz piece	26.4
Danish Pastry, cinnamon	2.5 oz piece	31.0
Danish Pastry, fruit	2.5 oz piece	33.9
Date, domestic, natural, pitted	10 dates	61.0
Dill Seed	1 tsp	1.2
Distilled, alc. (Gin, Rum, Vodka, Whiskey)		0.0
Dolphin Fish, no added ingredients		0.0
Donut, cake type, chocolate, frosted	1 medium	20.6
Donut, cake type, chocolate, glazed	1 medium	24.1
Donut, cruller, glazed	1 medium	24.4
Donut, yeast type, glazed	1 medium	26.6
Donut, yeast type, jelly filled	1 medium	33.2
Duck, no added ingredients		0.0
Egg, raw, whole	1 large	0.6
Egg, raw, white only	1 large	0.3
Egg, raw, yolk only	1 large	0.3
Egg, hard boiled, chopped	1 cup	1.4
Egg, substitute	¼ cup	1.0
Eggroll, wrapper	7" sq piece	18.5
Eggnog, nonalcoholic	1 cup	35.6
Eggplant, raw, with peel	1 cup	4.9
Eggplant, boiled	1 cup	6.5
Elderberries, raw	½ cup	13.2
Enchilada sauce	¼ cup	3.0
Endive, raw, chopped	½ cup	0.8
Fat, any animal		0.0
Fennel, bulb, raw	1 bulb	17.1
Fig, fresh	1 medium	9.6
Fig, canned, in heavy syrup	½ cup	29.7
Fig, dried	5 figs	61.1
Filberts or Hazelnuts, dry roasted	1 oz	5.0
Fish, breaded, frozen	1 oz stick	6.7
Fish Oil, any type		0.0
Flatfish (Flounder & Sole), no ingredients		0.0
Frankfurter, beef	1 link	0.9

Food	Serving size	Carb gm
Frankfurter, beef and pork	1 link	1.4
French beans, dried, boiled	½ cup	20.7
French toast, frozen	2.1 oz pce	19.0
Frosting, chocolate	2 tbsp	24.0
Fruit Cocktail, canned, heavy syrup	½ cup	24.2
Fruit Cocktail, canned, light syrup	½ cup	18.8
Fruit Cocktail, canned, juice	½ cup	14.7
Fruit Punch drink, frozen, diluted	1 oz	18.2
Fruit Salad, canned, heavy syrup	½ cup	29.8
Garlic	1 clove	1.0
Garlic Powder	1 tsp	2.3
Garlic, Salt	1 tsp	0.5
Gelatin Dessert Mix, flavored, prepared	½ cup	18.9
Gin & Tonic	1 fl oz	2.1
Ginger Ale	8 fl oz	21.6
Ginger, ground	1 tsp	1.2
Ginger Root, raw	¼ cup	3.6
Goose, no added ingredients		0.0
Gooseberries, raw	1 oz	7.6
Granola Bar, hard, plain	1 oz	18.3
Granola Bar, hard, chocolate chip	1 oz	20.4
Granola Bar, hard, peanut butter	1 oz	17.7
Granola Bar, soft, plain	1 oz	19.1
Granola Bar, soft, chocolate chip	1 oz	19.6
Granola Bar, soft, peanut butter	1 oz	18.2
Granola Bar, soft, raisin	1 oz	18.8
Grape, fresh, seedless	10 medium	8.9
Grape, fresh, slipskin	10 medium	4.1
Grape Drink, canned	8 fl oz	30.0
Grape Juice, canned or bottled	8 fl oz	38.0
Grape Soda	8 fl oz	27.2
Grapefruit, raw, pink or red	½ medium	10.6
Grapefruit, raw, white	½ medium	10.2
Grapefruit Juice, unsweetened	8 fl oz	22.2
Gravy, see specific listing		
Green Beans, fresh, raw	½ cup	3.9

Food	Serving size	Carb gm
Green Beans, fresh, boiled	½ cup	4.9
Green Pepper, sweet	1 medium	4.8
Grouper, no added ingredients		0.0
Haddock, no added ingredients		0.0
Halibut, no added ingredients		0.0
Ham, no added ingredients		0.0
Ham, lunch meat, minced	1 oz	0.5
Ham and Cheese Spread	1 tbsp	0.3
Hearts Of Palm, canned	1 cup	7.3
Hamburger patty, no added ingredients		0.0
Herring, fresh or canned		0.0
Herring, Atlantic, pickled	4 oz	10.9
Hollandaise Sauce Mix, dry	2 tbsp	2.0
Honey	1 tbsp	17.3
Honeydew Melon, cubed	½ cup	7.8
Horseradish, prepared	1 tbsp	1.0
Hot Dog, weiner only, no ingredients		0.0
Hubbard Squash, baked, cubed	½ cup	11.0
Hummus	2 tbsp	5.7
Ice Cream, chocolate	½ cup	18.6
Ice Cream, strawberry	½ cup	18.2
Ice Cream, vanilla	½ cup	15.5
Ice Milk, vanilla	½ cup	15.0
Italian Sausage, cooked, pork	1 link	1.7
Italian Seasoning	1 tsp	0.6
Jalapeno Dip	2 tbsp	3.0
Jam & Preserves, fruit	1 tbsp	12.9
Jelly, fruit	1 tbsp	13.5
Ketchup	1 tbsp	4.1
Kidney Beans, red	½ cup	20.1
Kiwi Fruit, fresh, raw	1 medium	11.4
Lamb, no added ingredients		0.0
Lard, pork		0.0
Leek, boiled	1 leek	9.9
Lemon	1 wedge	2.9
Lemon, peeled	2 " dia	5.4

Food	Serving size	Carb gm
Lemon Juice, fresh	1 tsp	0.4
Lemon-Lime Soda	8 fl oz	24.8
Lemon zest	1 tbsp	1.0
Lemonade, frozen, diluted	8 fl oz	24.8
Lentils, boiled	½ cup	19.9
Lettuce, Boston & Bibb, 1 head	5" dia	3.8
Lettuce, Boston & Bibb, inner leaves	2 leaves	0.4
Lettuce, Cos or Romaine, inner leaf	1 leaf	0.2
Lettuce, Iceberg	1 leaf	0.4
Lettuce, Looseleaf	1 Leaf	0.4
Lima Beans, boiled	½ cup	20.1
Lime, fresh	2" dia	7.4
Lime Juice, fresh	1 tsp	0.5
Limeade, frozen, diluted	8 fl oz	27.2
Ling cod, no added ingredients		0.0
Liqueur, coffee, 53 proof	1 fl oz	16.4
Liquor, (gin, rum, rye, scotch, vodka, etc.)		0.0
Liqueur, coffee, with cream, 34 proof	1 fl oz	6.5
Liver, beef, pan fried	4 oz	8.9
Liverwurst, pork	1 oz	0.6
Lobster, northern, meat only, boiled	4 oz	1.5
Loganberries, fresh	½ cup	10.9
Luncheon Meat, beef, thin sliced	1 oz	1.7
Luncheon Meat, pork	1 oz	0.6
Lychee, raw, shelled	1 oz	4.7
Macadamia Nuts, dried or oil roasted	1 oz	3.8
Macaroni, elbow, cooked	1 cup	39.7
Macaroni, small shells, cooked	1 cup	32.6
Macaroni, spirals, cooked	1 cup	38.0
Macaroni, vegetable, cooked	4 oz	30.2
Mace, ground	1 tsp	0.9
Mackerel, Atlantic, no added ingredients		0.0
Mahi Mahi, no added ingredients		0.0
Mangos, fresh, peeled, sliced	½ cup	14.0
Maple Syrup	¼ cup	52.9
Margarine, all types		0.0

Food	Serving size	Carb gm
Marjoram, dried	1 tsp	0.3
Marmalade, orange	1 tbsp	13.3
Marshmallow cream topping	1 fl oz	22.5
Martini, prepared from recipe	1 fl oz	0.1
Mayonnaise, real	1 tbsp	0.4
Mayonnaise, imitation, milk cream	1 tbsp	1.7
Mayonnaise, imitations, cholesterol free	1 tbsp	2.2
Melon Balls, mixed, frozen	1 cup	13.8
Melons, Cantaloupe, raw	1 cup	14.2
Melons, Honeydew, raw	1 cup	15.9
Milk, buttermilk, cultured,	1 cup	12.2
Milk, chocolate	1 cup	26.0
Milk, low fat, 2% fat	1 cup	11.7
Milk, skim	1 cup	11.9
Milk, whole, 3.3% fat	1 cup	11.4
Milk, canned, condensed, sweetened	1 tbsp	10.4
Milk, canned, evaporated, skim	1 tbsp	1.8
Milk, canned, evaporated, whole	1 tbsp	1.6
Milk, dry, whole	1 oz	10.9
Milk, dry, non fat, regular	¼ cup	15.6
Milk, dry, instant, packet	3.2 oz	35.5
Milk, goat	1 cup	9.8
Milk Shake, thick, chocolate	8 fl oz	47.2
Milk Shakes, thick, vanilla	8 fl oz	40.0
Milkfish, no added ingredients		0.0
Mixed Nuts, dry roasted, with peanuts	1 oz	7.2
Mixed Nuts, oil roasted, with peanuts	1 oz	6.1
Molasses	1 tbsp	13.8
Monkfish, no added ingredients		0.0
Muffin, blueberry	2 oz	27.4
Muffin, corn	2 oz	29.0
Muffin, English, plain	2 oz	28.2
Muffin, English, wheat	2 oz	25.5
Muffin, oat bran	2 oz	25.2
Muffin Mix, blueberry	1.75 oz	24.4
Muffin Mix, corn	1.75 oz	24.8

Food	Serving size	Carb gm
Muffin Mix, wheat bran	1.75 oz	23.3
Mulberry, raw	½ cup	7.0
Mushroom, raw	½ cup	1.6
Mushroom, boiled, pieces	½ cup	4.0
Mushroom, canned	½ cup	3.9
Mushroom, Shiitake, cooked, pieces	½ cup	10.4
Mushroom, Shiitake, dried	4 medium	11.3
Mushroom gravy, canned	¼ cup	3.0
Mussel, Blue, cooked, moist heat	3 oz	6.0
Mussel, Blue, raw	1 cup	6.0
Mustard, powder	1 tsp	0.3
Mustard, prepared	1 tsp	1.0
Mustard Greens, raw	1 cup	2.8
Mustard Greens, boiled, drained	1 cup	2.8
Mustard Seed, yellow	1 tsp	1.2
Navy Bean, boiled	½ cup	12.6
Nectarines, raw, medium	2½" dia	16.0
Noodle, egg, cooked	1 cup	39.7
Noodle, Chinese, dry, cellophane	2 oz	48.0
Noodle, Chinese, dry, chow mein	½ cup	13.0
Noodle, Japanese, cooked, soba	1 cup	24.4
Noodle, Japanese, cooked, somen	1 cup	48.5
Nutmeg, ground	1 tsp	1.1
Nuts, Mixed, dry roasted with peanuts	1 oz	7.2
Nuts, Mixed, oil roasted with peanuts	1 oz	6.1
Oat, whole grain, uncooked	½ cup	51.7
Oat, rolled or oatmeal, uncooked	½ cup	27.0
Oat, rolled or oatmeal, cooked	½ cup	22.5
Oat Bran, uncooked	½ cup	31.1
Oat Bran, cooked	½ cup	12.5
Oil, any type		0.0
Okra, fresh, boiled	½ cup	5.6
Okra, raw	1 cup	8.0
Olives, green, with pits	10 large	0.5
Olives, green, pitted	1 oz	0.4
Olives, ripe, Greek, with pits	10 medium	1.7

Food	Serving size	Carb gm
Onion, raw, chopped	½ cup	6.9
Onion, dried, minced	1 tsp	1.9
Onion, green, raw, chopped	½ cup	3.7
Onion Powder	1 tsp	2.4
Onion Rings, breaded	2 rings	7.6
Onion Salt	1 tsp	0.4
Orange, California, Navels	2" dia	16.3
Orange, California, Valencias	2" dia	14.4
Orange, Florida	2" dia	17.4
Orange, Mandarin	2" dia	9.4
Orange drink, canned or bottled	8 fl oz	32.0
Orange Juice, fresh	8 fl oz	25.6
Orange juice, canned or bottled	8 fl oz	24.8
Orange juice, frozen, diluted	8 fl oz	26.5
Oregano, ground	1 tsp	0.5
Oyster, Eastern, wild, cooked, moist heat	3 oz	6.6
Oyster, Eastern, wild, cooked, dry heat	3 oz	4.0
Oyster, Eastern, wild, raw, 6 medium	3 oz	3.3
Oyster, Pacific, cooked, moist heat	3 oz	8.4
Oyster, Pacific, raw	3 oz	4.2
Pancake, frozen, plain	4" cake	15.7
Pancake mix, prepared, plain	4" cake	11.0
Pancake mix, prepared, buckwheat	4" cake	8.5
Pancake mix, prepared, whole wheat	4" cake	13.0
Pancake Syrup	1 tbsp	15.1
Papaya, peeled, cubed	½ cup	7.0
Paprika	1 tsp	1.3
Parsley, dried	1 tbsp	0.6
Parsley, fresh	10 sprigs	0.6
Parsnip, boiled	½ cup	15.4
Passion Fruit, purple, raw	1 medium	4.2
Pasta, plain, cooked	1 cup	39.7
Pasta, corn, cooked	1 cup	39.1
Pasta, spinach, cooked	1 cup	36.6
Pasta, whole wheat	1 cup	37.2
Pasta Sauce, marinara	½ cup	12.7

Food	Serving size	Carb gm
Pasta Sauce, with mushrooms	½ cup	10.3
Pasta Sauce, with onions	½ cup	12.1
Pastrami, beef	1 oz	0.1
Pate, Chicken Liver	1 tbsp	0.9
Pate, Goose Liver, smoked	1 tbsp	0.6
Peach, fresh	2½" dia	9.7
Peach, fresh, peeled, pitted, sliced	2½" dia	9.4
Peach, canned, in juice	½ cup	14.3
Peach, canned, in light syrup	½ cup	18.3
Peach, canned, in heavy syrup	½ cup	25.5
Peach, dried, sulfured	½ cup	49.1
Peach Nectar, canned	8 fl oz	34.5
Peanut, shelled, unroasted	1 oz	4.5
Peanut, shelled, dry roasted	1 oz	6.0
Peanut, shelled, oil roasted	1 oz	5.3
Peanut, shelled, honey roasted	1 oz	8.0
Peanut Butter, chunky	1 tbsp	3.4
Peanut Butter, smooth	1 tbsp	3.3
Pear, Bartlett, fresh, with peel	1 medium	25.1
Pear, freshed sliced	½ cup	12.5
Pear, canned, halves in juice	½ cup	16.0
Pear, canned, halves in light syrup	½ cup	19.0
Pear, canned, halves in heavy syrup	½ cup	24.4
Pear, dried, sulfured	½ cup	62.7
Peas, edible pod (snow), fresh, raw	½ cup	5.4
Peas, edible pod (snow), fresh, boiled	½ cup	5.6
Peas, edible pod (snow), frozen, boiled	½ cup	7.2
Peas, green or sweet, fresh, raw	½ cup	10.4
Peas, green or sweet, fresh, boiled	½ cup	12.5
Peas, green or sweet, canned	½ cup	10.7
Peas, green or sweet, frozen, boiled	½ cup	16.2
Peas & Carrots, canned	½ cup	10.9
Peas & Carrots, frozen, boiled	½ cup	8.1
Peas & Onions, canned	½ cup	5.1
Peas & Onions, frozen, boiled	½ cup	7.8
Pecan, dried	1 oz	5.2

Food	Serving size	Carb gm
Pecan, dry roasted	1 oz	6.2
Pecan, oil roasted	1 oz	4.6
Pepper, black, whole	1 tsp	1.9
Pepper, black or white, ground	1 tsp	1.7
Pepper, red or cayenne	1 tsp	1.0
Pepper, chili, green or red, chopped	½ cup	7.1
Pepper, sweet, green or red, raw	1 medium	4.8
Pepper, sweet, yellow, raw	1 large	11.8
Pepper Sauce, hot		0.0
Peppermint, fresh	2 tbsp	0.4
Pepperoni, pork or beef	1 sausage	7.5
Perch, no added ingredients		0.0
Persimmons, Japanese, raw	1 fruit	31.9
Persimmons, Native, raw	1 fruit	8.5
Pheasant, no added ingredients		0.0
Picante Sauce (salsa)	2 tbsp	2.0
Pickle, cucumber, bread & butter	1 oz	6.0
Pickle, cucumber, dill	3¾" long	2.7
Pickle, cucumber, sour	3¾" long	0.8
Pickle, cucumber, sweet	3" long	11.1
Pickle Relish, hamburger	1 tbsp	5.1
Pickle Relish, hot dog	1 tbsp	3.4
Pickle Relish, sweet	1 tbsp	5.2
Pickling Spice	1 tsp	1.2
Pie, apple	⅛ of 9" pie	42.5
Pie, blueberry	⅛ of 9" pie	43.7
Pie, cherry	⅛ of 9" pie	49.8
Pie, chocolate cream	⅛ of 9" pie	31.9
Pie, coconut custard	⅛ of 9" pie	26.5
Pie, lemon meringue	⅛ of 9" pie	44.9
Pie, peach	⅛ of 9" pie	32.4
Pie, pecan	⅛ of 9" pie	58.0
Pie, pumpkin	⅛ of 9" pie	26.7
Pie Crust, frozen	9" shell	62.7
Pie Crust, mix, prepared	9" shell	80.7
Pike, Northern, no added ingredients		0.0

Food	Serving size	Carb gm
Pimento, canned	1 oz	1.0
Pina Colada, prepared from recipe	8 fl oz	69.6
Pine Nuts, pignolia, dried	1 oz	4.0
Pine Nuts, pinyon, dried	1 oz	5.4
Pineapple, raw, diced	½ cup	9.3
Pineapple, canned, juice	½ cup	19.6
Pineapple, canned, light syrup	½ cup	16.9
Pineapple, canned, heavy syrup	½ cup	25.8
Pineapple Juice, canned or bottled	8 fl oz	34.4
Pistachio Nuts, dried, shelled	1 oz	7.1
Pistachio Nuts, dry roasted, shelled	1 oz	7.8
Plums, raw, pitted, sliced	½ cup	10.7
Plums, Japanese	2" dia	8.6
Plums, canned, juice	½ cup	19.1
Plums, canned, light syrup	½ cup	20.5
Plums, canned, heavy syrup	½ cup	30.0
Polish Sausage, pork	1 oz	0.6
Pollock, no added ingredients		0.0
Pomegranates, raw	1 fruit	26.2
Popcorn, air popped	1 cup	6.2
Popcorn, oil popped	1 cup	6.3
Popcorn, carmel coated with peanuts	2 oz	45.7
Poppy Seed	1 tbsp	2.2
Pork, no added ingredients		0.0
Pork rind snack, plain	1 oz	0.0
Pork rind snack, barbeque	1 oz	0.5
Potato, baked in skin	1 medium	51.0
Potato, baked without skin	½ cup	13.2
Potato, boiled	½ cup	27.2
Potato, mashed with whole milk	½ cup	18.4
Potato, mashed, whole milk & butter	½ cup	17.5
Potato, frozen, french fried, oven heated	10 strips	17.0
Potato, frozen, fried, cottage cut	4 oz	38.6
Potato, frozen, hash brown, cooked in oil	½ cup	21.9
Potato, mix, mashed flakes, prepared	½ cup	15.8
Potato, sweet (see "Sweet Potato")		

Food	Serving size	Carb gm
Potato Chips	1 oz	14.7
Potato Pancakes, home prepared	1 pancake	22.0
Poultry Seasoning	1 tsp	0.9
Pretzels	1 oz	22.0
Prune Juice	8 fl oz	43.5
Prunes, canned, heavy syrup	5 medium	23.9
Prunes, dried, dehydrated, uncooked	½ cup	58.8
Pudding, ready to eat, banana	5 oz	30.1
Pudding, ready to eat, chocolate	5 oz	32.4
Pudding, ready to eat, lemon	5 oz	35.6
Pudding, ready to eat, rice	5 oz	31.3
Pudding, ready to eat, tapioca	5 oz	27.5
Pudding, ready to eat, vanilla	5 oz	29.8
Pudding Mix, with milk, banana, instant	½ cup	29.0
Pudding Mix, with milk, banana, regular	½ cup	25.3
Pudding Mix, with milk, chocolate, instant	½ cup	27.8
Pudding Mix, with milk, chocolate, regular	½ cup	25.5
Pudding Mix, with milk, coconut crm, inst	½ cup	28.0
Pudding Mix, with milk, coconut crm, reg	½ cup	24.7
Pudding Mix, with milk, lemon, instant	½ cup	29.5
Pudding Mix, with milk, rice	½ cup	30.0
Pudding Mix, with milk, tapioca	½ cup	27.6
Pudding Mix, with milk, vanilla, instant	½ cup	27.9
Pudding Mix, with milk, vanilla, regular	½ cup	26.0
Puff Pastry, frozen	1.4 oz shell	18.3
Pumpkin, pulp, boiled, mashed	½ cup	6.0
Pumpkin Pie Mix, canned	½ cup	35.1
Pumpkin Pie Spice	1 tsp	1.2
Quail, no added ingredients		0.0
Radicchio, raw, shredded	½ cup	0.8
Radish	10 medium	1.6
Radishes, Oriental, raw, sliced	½ cup	1.8
Radishes, white icicle, sliced	½ cup	1.3
Raisins, Golden Seedless, not packed	¼ cup	28.9
Raisins, seedless, not packed	¼ cup	28.7
Ranch Dip	2 tbsp	3.0

Food	Serving size	Carb gm
Raspberries, fresh	½ cup	7.1
Raspberries, frozen, sweetened	½ cup	32.7
Red Snapper, no added ingredients		0.0
Refried Beans, canned	½ cup	23.3
Rhubarb, frozen, uncooked, diced	1 cup	6.8
Rhubarb, frozen, cooked, with sugar	1 cup	74.4
Rhubarb, raw, unsweetened, diced	½ cup	2.8
Rice, cooked, brown, long grain	½ cup	22.5
Rice, cooked, white, long grain	½ cup	22.3
Rice, precooked or inst, white, long grain	½ cup	17.4
Rice Bran	⅓ cup	13.9
Rice Flour, brown	½ cup	60.4
Rice Flour, white	½ cup	63.3
Rice Mix, with pasta and seasoning	½ cup	21.7
Roll, commercial, dinner	1 oz	14.3
Roll, commercial, dinner, rye	1 oz	15.1
Roll, commercial, dinner, wheat	1 oz	13.0
Roll, commercial, French	1.3 oz	19.1
Roll, commercial, hamburger or hot dog	1.5 oz	21.6
Roll, commercial, hard or kaiser	2 oz	30.1
Root Beer	8 fl oz	27.2
Rosemary, dried	1 tsp	0.7
Rutabagas, boiled	½ cup	7.4
Rutabaga, raw, cubed	½ cup	5.6
Safflower Seed kernels, dried	1 oz	9.5
Safflower Seed meal, partially defatted	1 oz	13.7
Saffron	1 tsp	0.5
Sage, ground	1 tsp	0.4
Salad Dressing, 1000 Island	2 tbsp	4.8
Salad Dressing, Blue Cheese	2 tbsp	2.2
Salad Dressing, Caesar	2 tbsp	2.0
Salad Dressing, French	2 tbsp	5.4
Salad Dressing, French, low calorie	2 tbsp	7.0
Salad Dressing, Italian	2 tbsp	3.0
Salad Dressing, Mayonnaise	2 tbsp	7.0
Salad Dressing, Russian	2 tbsp	3.2

Food	Serving size	Carb gm
Salad Dressing, Russian, low calorie	2 tbsp	9.0
Salad Dressing, Sesame Seed	2 tbsp	2.6
Salami, beef	1 oz	0.7
Salami, beef & pork	1 oz	0.6
Salmon, fresh, canned, smoked		0.0
Salsa	2 tbsp	2.0
Salt, table		0.0
Sandwich Spread, beef & pork	1 tbsp	1.8
Sandwich Spread, meatless	1 tbsp	3.4
Sardine, fresh or canned in oil		0.0
Sauerkraut, canned with liquid	½ cup	5.1
Sausage, pork, cooked	1 link	0.1
Sausage, pork & beef, cooked	1 link	0.8
Savory, ground	1 tsp	1.0
Scallop, meat only	2 lrg or 5 sm	0.6
Screwdriver, prepared from recipe	1 fl oz	2.7
Sea Bass, no added ingredients		0.0
Sesame flour, partially defatted	1 oz	10.0
Sesame meal, partially defatted	1 oz	7.4
Sesame seeds, whole, roasted	1 oz	7.3
Shad, no added ingredients		0.0
Shallots, fresh, chopped	1 tbsp	1.7
Sherbet, orange	½ cup	29.2
Sherbet Bar, orange	2.75 fl oz	20.1
Shortening, any type		0.0
Shrimp, meat only, raw	4 oz	1.0
Shrimp, canned, drained	1 cup	1.3
Shrimp, imitation from surimi	4 oz	10.4
Snapper, no added ingredients		0.0
Soft Drinks, carbonated, club soda	12 fl oz	0.0
Soft Drinks, carbonated, cola	12 fl oz	42.0
Soft Drinks, carbonated, cola, diet	12 fl oz	0.0
Soft Drinks, carbonated, ginger ale	12 fl oz	38.0
Soft Drinks, carbonated, orange	12 fl oz	52.0
Soft Drinks, carbonated, root beer	12 fl oz	43.0
Soft Drinks, carbonated, tonic	12 fl oz	36.0

Food	Serving size	Carb gm
Sole, no added ingredients		0.0
Sorbet, raspberry	½ cup	30.0
Soup, canned, ready, bean/ham, chunky	1 cup	27.1
Soup, canned, ready, beef	1 cup	19.6
Soup, canned, ready, beef/chicken broth	1 cup	0.1
Soup, canned, ready, chicken, chunky	1 cup	17.3
Soup, canned, ready, chicken noodle	1 cup	8.4
Soup, canned, ready, chicken vegetable	1 cup	18.9
Soup, canned, ready, clam chowder	1 cup	18.8
Soup, canned, ready, crab	1 cup	10.3
Soup, canned, ready, lentil with ham	1 cup	20.2
Soup, canned, ready, minestrone, chunky	1 cup	20.7
Soup, canned, ready, vegetable, chunky	1 cup	19.0
Soup, canned, with water, black bean	1 cup	19.8
Soup, canned, with water, bean & bacon	1 cup	22.8
Soup, canned, with water, beef bouillon	1 cup	1.0
Soup, canned, with water, beef noodle	1 cup	9.0
Soup, canned, with water, cheese	1 cup	10.5
Soup, canned, with water, chicken broth	1 cup	0.9
Soup, canned, with water, chicken dump	1 cup	6.0
Soup, canned, with water, chicken gumbo	1 cup	8.4
Soup, canned, with water, chicken noodle	1 cup	9.4
Soup, canned, with water, chicken rice	1 cup	7.2
Soup, canned, with water, chicken veg	1 cup	8.6
Soup, canned, with water, chili beef	1 cup	21.5
Soup, canned, with water, clam chowder	1 cup	12.2
Soup, canned, with water, green pea	1 cup	26.5
Soup, canned, with water, minestrone	1 cup	11.2
Soup, canned, with water, mushroom	1 cup	11.2
Soup, canned, with water, onion	1 cup	8.2
Soup, canned, with water, oyster stew	1 cup	9.8
Soup, canned, with water, Scotch broth	1 cup	9.5
Soup, canned, with water, tomato	1 cup	16.6
Soup, canned, with water, tomato noodle	1 cup	21.2
Soup, canned, with water, tomato rice	1 cup	21.9
Soup, canned, with water, turkey noodle	1 cup	8.6

Food	Serving size	Carb gm
Soup, canned, with water, vegetable beef	1 cup	10.2
Soup, canned, with water, vegetable	1 cup	13.0
Soup, mix, with water, beef bouillon	1 cup	1.9
Soup, mix, with water, beef noodle	1 cup	6.0
Soup, mix, with water, cauliflower	1 cup	10.7
Soup, mix, with water, chicken, cream of	1 cup	13.4
Soup, mix, with water, chicken bouillon	1 cup	1.4
Soup, mix, with water, chicken noodle	1 cup	7.4
Soup, mix, with water, chicken rice	1 cup	9.3
Soup, mix, with water, chicken vegetable	1 cup	7.8
Soup, mix, with water, leek	1 cup	11.4
Soup, mix, with water, minestrone	1 cup	11.9
Soup, mix, with water, mushroom	1 cup	11.1
Soup, mix, with water, onion	1 cup	5.1
Soup, mix, with water, pea, green or split	1 cup	22.7
Soup, mix, with water, tomato or cream of	1 cup	19.4
Soup, mix, with water, vegetable beef	1 cup	8.0
Sour Cream, regular	2 tbsp	1.0
Sour Cream, non fat	2 tbsp	4.0
Soy flour, full fat roasted	1 cup	28.6
Soy flour, defatted	1 cup	38.4
Soy meal, defatted, raw	1 cup	49.0
Soy milk	8 fl oz	4.3
Soy protein, concentrate	1 oz	8.8
Soy sauce, tamari	1 tbsp	1.0
Soybean, green, raw, shelled	½ cup	14.1
Soybean, green, boiled	½ cup	10.0
Soybean, dried, boiled	½ cup	8.5
Soybean, roasted	½ cup	28.9
Spaghetti Squash, baked or broiled	½ cup	5.0
Spareribs, no added ingredients		0.0
Spinach, fresh, raw, chopped	½ cup	1.0
Spinach, fresh, boiled	½ cup	3.4
Spinach, frozen, leaf, boiled	½ cup	5.1
Split Peas, boiled	½ cup	20.7
Squash, Summer, all varieties, sliced	½ cup	2.3

Food	Serving size	Carb gm
Strawberry, fresh	½ cup	5.2
Strawberry, canned in heavy syrup	½ cup	29.9
Strawberry, frozen, unsweetened	½ cup	6.8
Strawberry milk drink mix, dry	1 oz	28.1
Stuffing, mix, dry, bread	1 oz	21.6
Stuffing, mix, dry, corn bread	1 oz	21.8
Sturgeon, no added ingredients		0.0
Succotash, canned, cream style corn	½ cup	23.4
Succotash, canned, whole kernel corn	½ cup	17.9
Succotash, frozen, boiled	½ cup	17.0
Sugar, beet or cane, granulated	1 tbsp	12.0
Sugar, maple	1 oz	25.5
Sugar substitute	1 packet	<1.0
Sunflower Seed, kernels, dried	1 oz	5.3
Sunflower Seed, kernels, dry roasted	1 oz	6.8
Sunflower Seed, kernels, oil roasted	1 oz	4.2
Sunflower Seed, kernels, toasted	1 oz	5.9
Sweet Potato, baked in skin	1 medium	27.7
Sweet Potato, baked in skin, mashed	½ cup	24.3
Sweet Potato, boiled, no skin	4 oz	27.5
Sweet Potato, boiled, no skin, mashed	½ cup	39.8
Sweet & Sour Sauce	1 tbsp	7.0
Swiss Chard, raw, chopped	½ cup	0.7
Swiss Chard, boiled, chopped	½ cup	3.6
Swordfish, no added ingredients		0.0
Taco shell	1 average	6.3
Tangerine, fresh	1 medium	9.4
Tangerine, canned, juice	½ cup	11.9
Tangerine, canned, light syrup	½ cup	20.4
Tapioca, dry, pearl	1 oz	25.1
Tarragon, ground	1 tsp	0.8
Tartar Sauce	2 tbsp	1.0
Tea, regular or herbal		0.0
Thyme, ground	1 tsp	0.9
Tofu, fresh	½ cup	2.3
Tofu, okara	½ cup	5.4

Food	Serving size	Carb gm
Tom Collins, prepared from recipe	1 fl oz	0.3
Tomato, fresh, raw	1 medium	5.7
Tomato, fresh, boiled	½ cup	7.0
Tomato, dried	½ cup	15.1
Tomato, canned, whole	½ cup	5.2
Tomato Juice	8 fl oz	10.0
Tomato Paste	1 tbsp	3.0
Tomato puree	¼ cup	6.0
Tomato Sauce, canned, regular	½ cup	8.8
Tomato Sauce, with onions	½ cup	12.1
Tonic Water	8 fl oz	21.6
Trail Mix, regular, plain, chocolate chips	1 oz	12.7
Trout, no added ingredients		0.0
Tuna, no added ingredients		0.0
Turkey, no added ingredients		0.0
Turkey gravy, canned	¼ cup	3.5
Turmeric, ground	1 tsp	1.5
Turnip, boiled, chopped	½ cup	3.8
Turnip, boiled, mashed	½ cup	5.6
Turnip Greens, fresh, raw, chopped	½ cup	1.6
Turnip Greens, fresh, boiled, chopped	½ cup	3.1
Vanilla Extract, no alcohol	1 tsp	0.6
Veal, no added ingredients		0.0
Vegetable juice	8 fl oz	10.0
Vegetables, mixed, canned	½ cup	8.7
Vegetables, mixed, frozen	½ cup	11.9
Venison, no added ingredients		0.0
Vinegar	1 tbsp	1.0
Waffle, frozen, plain or buttermilk	4" square	13.5
Walnut, Black, dried	1 oz	3.4
Walnut, English or Persian, dried	1 oz	5.2
Water, Bottled		0.0
Waterchestnuts, Chinese, raw	4 medium	8.6
Waterchestnuts, Chinese, fresh, sliced	½ cup	14.8
Watercress	10 sprigs	0.3
Watermelon, 1" thick slice	10" dia	34.6

Food	Serving size	Carb gm
Whiskey Sour, prepared from recipe	1 fl oz	1.8
Wheat, whole grain	¼ cup	34.2
Wheat bran	2 tbsp	6.0
Wheat flour, all purpose white	¼ cup	23.9
Wheat flour, cake, white	¼ cup	21.3
Wheat flour, whole grain	¼ cup	21,8
Wheat germ	1 oz	14.7
White Bean, dried, boiled	½ cup	22.6
Whitefish, no added ingredients		0.0
Wild Rice, cooked	½ cup	17.5
Wine, dessert or apertif	4 fl oz	9.2
Wine, table or dry	4 fl oz	4.8
Worcestershire sauce	1 tsp	1.0
Yam, fresh, baked or boiled	½ cup	18.8
Yeast, Baker's	¼ oz pkg	2.7
Yellow Beans, dried, boiled	½ cup	22.2
Yogurt, plain, whole milk	8 fl oz	10.6
Yogurt, plain, low fat	8 fl oz	16.0
Yogurt, plain, nonfat	8 fl oz	17.4
Yogurt, frozen, chocolate, soft serve	½ cup	17.9
Yogurt, frozen, vanilla, soft serve	½ cup	17.4
Zucchini, fresh, raw, sliced	½ cup	1.9
Zucchini, fresh, boiled, sliced	½ cup	3.5
Zucchini, fresh, boiled, mashed	½ cup	7.8

Index

ISBN 155369376-0

9 781553 693765